# It's Your Life,

## Live it,

### Love It!

*A guide to improving emotional health.*

By

Julie W. Hubbs, M.S.

Second edition 2017

ISBN: 978-1-941125-76-2

Library of Congress Control Number: 2016951480

Hubbs, Julie W.
    *It's Your Life, live It, Love It.* Julie W. Hubbs.

Cover designers: Kymberly Loya and Lacey Taylor.
Cover Photographer: Julie W. Hubbs, M.S.

Some names in this book have been changed out of respect for the people's privacy.

With love to my husband Tom.

# Table of Contents

# Introduction

In *It's Your Life, Live It, Love It!* I tell you the story of my life and the problems that I have overcome with the hopes that you too can overcome any challenges in your life. As a child I grew up believing all people were loving and kind. What I learned in my early twenties is that some people are just mean and cruel. As a young woman, I did not have the knowledge, skills, ability, or self-confidence to stand up to bullies who were trying to control me. I made up excuses for their bad behaviors because I needed to believe there was something good in everyone. Perhaps I needed to see something good in everyone so I could feel better about my own life.

I mistakenly trusted everyone, and this nearly cost me my life. Although my physical scars have long ago healed, because of my past abuse I can still become anxious when I am feeling trapped or controlled by another person. The difference now is I have life skills that allow me to make healthier choices for myself, and I am no longer a victim without a voice.

I believe it is important for you to hear my story and how I became determined to make life changes for myself that allowed me to live the life I deserve.

We have one life to live so we might as well love it.

# Chapter 1

# Childhood

When I grew up in Fair Oaks, California, there were no alcoholics. Also, husbands and wives were kind to one another, and no one used, let alone abused drugs. All children were treated with kindness and respect. Neighbors always got along, and life was beautiful and peaceful. If you believe all of that, I have a bridge to sell you.

This is a story of how despair and dysfunction became hope and thriving. I hope my journey will inspire you.

My mom, Georgianna, was born in 1934 in Sacramento. My maternal grandfather, Frank Millas, was a hardworking Greek immigrant who owned several restaurants in downtown Sacramento. My maternal grandmother, Florence, divorced my grandfather when my mom was about six years old. Later, she married and divorced a few more times and ended up owning and running her own bar near downtown.

Frank and Florence had three daughters. Mom was the oldest. Then came her two sisters, Genevieve and Patricia. When I was a child, Mom would let me talk on the telephone to my aunts, but only on holidays. I was allowed to say hello and then tell them how I was doing in school. After a few minutes, Mom would take the phone from my ear and end the conversation with her sisters. My mom was not interested in having a family relationship with any of her family members after the death of her father.

I never met my biological grandparents. Well, that is not exactly true. I never met Frank because he died before I was born, but I did finally see my grandmother at my Aunt Genevieve's funeral when I was 37 years old. I first saw my grandmother from across the room at the mortuary. Florence, who by then was in the advanced stages of Alzheimer's, seemed to recognize my mom's voice and became very agitated. Without any warning, she grabbed Mom's neck and refused to let go. My mom was frightened and crying, and then she began to have a panic attack. We were able to separate the two, and eventually Mom and Florence both calmed down. Because of all the turmoil, the rest of Florence's family did not think she needed to be introduced to me.

After the funeral, we all went to the cemetery for the graveside service. Mom and I were told to sit in the first row in front of the casket. Mom sat down and I sat next to her. Then Florence was seated in the empty seat on my other side. I must admit having my mother on my right and my grandmother on my left for the first time in my life, felt strange. I found myself comparing our complexions, skin textures, and the shapes of our arms. I tried hard to find family resemblances and memorize everything I could. I had never seen my grandmother before, but my mom had told me on several occasions that I looked like Florence. I wanted to take full advantage of this opportunity because I thought it was unlikely that I would ever see my grandmother again.

As I was leaving the cemetery, I overheard people saying they needed to get Florence back to Norwood Pines. My ears perked up because I was working for Yolo County Mental Health Services at the time, and I often had clients who were living at the Norwood Pines Care Center, I was mandated to see my clients face to face at least twice monthly, and I was due for a visit to that facility soon.

When I arrived at the Care Center for that mandated visit, I signed in and told the woman at the front desk who I was visiting. On a whim, I added Florence's name to the visitor's sheet. I wasn't sure if she actually resided at this Center, and if she did live there, whether I could get a visit with her, but I added her name to the list anyway.

The Center cared for many Alzheimer's and mental health patients, housed in separate sections; therefore, the facility was locked and visitors needed a good reason to go inside. I was nervous about having Florence's name on the visitor's list. Then the woman at the front desk shrieked and said, "Oh good, Florence doesn't get any visitors. I'm glad you are seeing her, and I'm sure she'll love it." With that being said, she hit the buzzer. The door opened, and I was inside with a copy of the visitor's list of residents I was scheduled to see.

I always scheduled this Center's visits at the end of my work day because it was on my way home. My plan was to see Florence after seeing my clients. Usually the visits with my clients went well because they enjoyed talking with me, and I brought them their favorite cookies or bags of chips.

This particular week both of my clients refused to talk to me. Both were extremely agitated, and they only wanted their treats. The visits took longer than usual because I had to meet with the nurses afterward to assess how my clients were doing. I was mentally exhausted by the time I was done. I wondered if my clients were sensing my nervousness regarding Florence, making them more difficult than usual.

It had been a long day. I was so tired I just wanted to go home before the commute traffic got bad. I decided I would see Florence the next time I came for a visit. A nurse passed me in the hallway, and I asked her for directions to the Alzheimer's unit. I wanted to be prepared for the next visit which would include Florence. The nurse said that unit was on the other side of the building and offered to walk me over there.

I felt it would be rude to tell her no thank you, so I followed her down the hallway. She asked who I was visiting, and I told her Florence. Then she stopped and said "Oh! Florence is right here, and she's a sweetheart." I looked into a large room to see a very old woman in a hospital bed. She seemed to be sleeping. There were a few personal items on a nearby shelf.

My feet wouldn't move, and I stood there staring, afraid to go in. I was beginning to think I had no business intruding into the private and personal life of a woman I knew only through my bloodline. My mom had purposely kept me isolated from her past, which included Florence. Mom always tried her best to keep me emotionally and physically protected, and here I was at the doorway of my mom's personal hell.

The nurse again encouraged me to go in and have my visit. I slowly walked in and stared at the beautiful, sleeping woman. The nurse brought me a chair and said, "She can hear you, but she can't speak. She's in the advanced stages." I asked if she seemed to understand what went on around her, and the nurse said, "I believe she does." With that she left the room. I was alone for the first time in my life with my grandmother.

Within about 10 minutes, a second nurse came charging in demanding to know who I was. I told her, "It's complicated." I explained my job as a mental health clinician, told her I had clients in the building I see twice a month, and I had just learned Florence was living in the same facility as my clients.

I then told her I was Florence's first biological grandchild and that Florence didn't know me, and I didn't know her. I refused to go into all the family drama with a stranger. I made it clear I was not going to check on people who were on my caseload and not check on my own family member when she resided in the building. This nurse did not seem satisfied with my answers, but she nodded and walked out the door. About 15 minutes later, she came back to advise me she had called Florence's daughter Peggy, and I was cleared to visit anytime I desired.

By the time I left that night I was drained, but I knew I must tell my mom about the visit with Florence. If this upset Mom, I would never visit Florence again. My mom had made great efforts to keep herself and me physically and emotionally safe from her dysfunctional family, and I was not willing to cause her harm in any way.

I drove straight over to the family home, told Mom what happened, and she said, "That's very nice of you. She's just a little old lady now. What happened has already happened. If you want to visit her again, then do it. I am sure her family would appreciate it." I asked her if she would like to see Florence again. Mom paused, looked into my eyes and said "No! I have no need."

Does this all sound a little crazy? It should sound a little crazy because it is crazy! Let me back up. I bet you have already figured out Mom came from a highly dysfunctional family. After Frank and Florence divorced, Mom was pretty much neglected and left on her own. Florence began hanging out at her bar, flirting with men and doing a lot of drinking. Mom, at the age of six, was left to care for her two younger sisters. In addition to the neglect, she was being abused physically, emotionally, and sexually. In 1944, at the age of 10, Mom was removed from her mother's home and sent to a foster home in Fair Oaks.

At this time, Fair Oaks was a small semi-rural town about 15 miles east of Sacramento. It was just starting to change from farms and orchards to a more suburban population with the influx of defense workers and military from Sacramento's two Air Force bases and Army Depot who needed affordable housing. With a good foster family and a safe place to live, it must have seemed like paradise to Mom.

By age 15, she was reunited with her father Frank. She now attended a Catholic all-girls school and worked as a waitress in his family restaurant.

While in foster care, Mom met my dad Stan. Dad's parents were both immigrants from Czechoslovakia, and he was the youngest of five children.

Mom always talked about how big and handsome Stan was. She also liked that he came from a large family. Two of his three brothers and his sister were married and had children. My mom adored Stan's parents and very much wanted them to be her in-laws. She was madly in love with Stan.

Growing up without much parental supervision and living in foster care, Mom always craved a family of her own. She was married at age 17 before she graduated from high school. Her father Frank really liked Stan, and thought he was a good solid man who would take care of his daughter. Frank also believed

Mom would be safe with my dad, especially since they would be living close to my dad's family. Less than two years after Mom and Dad married, my Grandpa Frank had a heart attack and died instantly at the age of 54. I am not sure Mom ever really recovered from the death of her father.

Five years into their marriage, when Mom was 22 years old, I came along via C-section. My parents had to scrimp and save to pay for my birth because there was no maternity insurance. Before Mom left the hospital she made a vow to herself, "To be the best mom, to protect her children from emotional and physical abuse, and to use Dr. Spock's book as her parental bible."

Mom and Dad, with the help of my paternal grandfather Joseph, built a modest two bedroom, one bathroom house on a narrow country lane near my dad's folks. It was directly across the street from Lewis and Thelma Wolf who eventually became my godparents.

"Thelma's Beauty Shop" was located inside the Wolf home. My dad and grandpa had previously enclosed Thelma's breezeway between the house and the garage and built her a two chair beauty shop. The beauty shop became the gathering place for the local women. There always fresh coffee in the peculator and homemade cookies in the cookie jar for anyone who stopped by.

It is no secret that when women gather together they talk about anything and everything. For the longest time, Mom said she would listen quietly to what the "older" ladies were saying. They all seemed perfect to her. At age 22 with a new baby, being a graduate of the foster care system and having no parents to offer guidance, Mom was feeling far from perfect. Her feelings of being constantly overwhelmed kept her studying Dr. Spock's book, "The Common Sense Book of Baby and Child Care."

Mom, being so overwhelmed, eventually softened on the idea of trying to be the perfect mother. As time passed, she started feeling more comfortable in her community, and she felt we were all physically and emotionally safe. It didn't hurt that Mom had banned her mother Florence from having any contact with her, me or any future children. Florence wasn't that interested in us anyway, so in Mom's mind we were all safe, and all was good.

What Mom didn't count on, was the fact that there were alcoholics in Fair Oaks, people did get into drugs, husbands and wives could be nasty to one another, and some of her friends were abusing their children right there in the town that seemed so perfect to her.

Mom spent a great deal of time listening to other people's problems. She enjoyed learning about their situations and tried to help them in any way she could. Mom wanted and needed to feel loved and accepted. She would get close to people, but she listened to her own gut instinct, and she was often slow to completely trust. Once you were her friend, she was your friend for life. Some of her best friends, at the end of her life, were friends she met in high school or early in her real estate career. Mom never gave up on people she cared about, and in the end they did not give up on her.

After I was born, my parents and Grandpa Joseph started building a bigger family home for us. The new house had three bedrooms, two bathrooms, a living room, dining room, and a family room. It also had a two car attached garage. When I was two, we moved to our new house near the American River. The neighbors on either side of us had also built their homes themselves.

Money was tight in the 1950s, but sweat equity was cheap. The three families became very close. So close in fact that if you misbehaved at one house, you were punished before you made it home to your house. If you needed a bath, you were cleaned up, and if you scraped your knee, you had a bandage and a reassuring hug right on the spot. Talk about growing up in my own little utopia.

As I mentioned earlier, money was tight in the 1950s and 1960s. The families on our side of the street all had nearly acre lots. The houses were built close to the street which meant we had huge back yards to play in. Every house was designed and built with very large windows overlooking the yards.

Mom said her house was designed so she could always keep an eye on her children. She wanted her children to be free to play, but she also had a strong need to know what we were doing at all times and that we were safe. Mom strongly valued independence, creativity, and fun. She loved free play using imaginations but always had a need to keep an eye on us.

No one had gardeners in those days. Thank goodness our parents enjoyed yard work. I guess they must have since they bought such large lots. Grass was planted, then mowed by our dads. Can you imagine being a kid and having acres of grass to play on? We truly grew up in heaven on earth, if you ask me.

In December 1960, two years after moving into our new house, my sister Anna was born. By this time Mom had nearly ten years of marriage under her belt. Dr. Spock's book had long ago been donated to charity, and Mom had let go of just being the best mom. Instead, she had expanded her goals to be the best wife, best homemaker, and the best mom. Are you starting to see a trend here? Mom always had a need to be extra good at things. She needed people to love her. She needed to feel good enough. This is not at all uncommon for people who were abused as children and were abandoned by their loved ones.

Expending energy trying to be the best at everything did not allow room to discuss dangerous situations. Oh, mom taught us about stranger danger and she made sure we knew about inappropriate touching, but that is about as far as the training went. In the 1950s, 1960s, and 1970s, everyone knew everyone in Fair Oaks. My grandpa Joseph was the constable and when he got older, he became the night watchman. We knew everyone, and everyone knew us.

By the middle 1960's there were six kids who lived on our side of the street, four girls and two boys. Lynn and Kate were the oldest girls. Kurt, Brad and I were in the middle, and my little sister Anna was the youngest. Her friends were on the other side of the street after families with younger children moved in.

As we grew older, playing on plain grass became a bit boring. Our parents got creative and started collecting free scrap wood from the scrap box at the Fair Oaks Lumber and Hardware Store. Before we knew it, we had two play houses equipped with cabinets, flooring, doors, shingle roofs, wooden tables and chairs, curtains, and boxes of dress up clothes to play with.

The play houses were on the back part of the lots and were about 12'x12'. Over the years those play houses became forts, bunkers, stores, restaurants, craft rooms, cabins, hotels, and places to hide in the night during our many kick the can games.

Ed, who lived to our left, built what we called "The Platform." Today we would call it a play structure. Ed was a terrific designer. The platform had bars to swing on, places to climb and jump from, and an opening to fly out of as you jumped onto a rope swing. Later he added a tether ball court, a sandbox, and a canvas hammock that was bolted into two trees. The hammock was a perfect setup for swinging a kid in 360 degree motion while being wrapped inside.

My dad was not wanting to be upstaged, so he built a second tether ball court on our property and added a regulation size volleyball court with a tournament size net. Later a horseshoe pit would be added to the mix.

One day Ed came home with some large wooden spools from the telephone company. We were so excited to have some new yard toys. Ed spruced them up and changed them to look like different sized barrels. We played with those barrels for over a decade, staging races and contests. We included my little sister Anna and the younger kids across the street.

Over the years, all five families from both sides of the street became very close. More than fifty years later we are still very close. Many of the parents have since died. My mom was the last living neighborhood mom. When she passed away in March 2014, all the neighborhood kids attended her memorial.

Our parents had a strong belief in keeping their children safe. My mom loved it best when our friends came to our house. She wanted to give us freedom, but under a watchful eye. Mom made sure we felt safe, secure, and loved at all times because she did not grow up feeling emotionally safe. No one was there to protect and care for her when she was little. She made it her mission in life to make sure her children never felt abandoned. Mom had a firsthand view of what true abandonment looked and felt like, and she never

13

wanted us to have that experience.

Our neighborhood was a fantastic place to grow up. All of us kids thought we were rich. We grew up in great houses and had large park like settings to play in every single day of our childhood. We all got along like siblings. Yes we had fights, squabbled, whined, and tattled on each other, but there was no hatred, just love.

As the years went on, the five sets of neighbors on both sides of the street kept getting closer and closer. Mom was not comfortable with her children calling the adults by their first names. Everyone became my aunt or uncle. To our right was Auntie Jean and Uncle Bill. To our left was Uncle Ed and Mary Helen (I guess her name was too long to be an aunt). Across the street on the right was Momma Shannon (her daughter's name was also Shannon) and Uncle Mike. To the left across the street was Auntie Nora and Uncle Keigi.

Nora and Keigi were Japanese Americans who had spent some time in the internment camps during World War II. Mom and Auntie Nora became very close friends. They were both interested in the arts, ceramics, and were excellent seamstresses.

On several occasions Mom and Auntie Nora would pile us kids into the car for a road trip to San Francisco. Their goal was to study and sketch the latest fashions in the store windows to reproduce later at home. We always made a visit to the Japanese Tea Garden in Golden Gate Park. There was nothing

14

better than seeing the beautiful grounds while we ate our picnic lunches.

We always stopped at the gift store to pick up some Japanese jelly candies wrapped in rice paper that melts in your mouth. Mom and Auntie Nora both believed in taking advantage of every possible learning opportunity. Strolling through the park was an excellent way for us kids to learn about the Japanese culture. I loved the Japanese culture so much that my goal in life was to grow up and be Japanese. The closest I came to that goal was a time when Auntie Nora dressed me and Anna up for Halloween in Kimonos and fixed our hair using fancy hair decorations. I felt like a Japanese princess.

Another exciting part of these road trips was stopping at the Nut Tree for a fancy lunch. The Nut Tree was located in Vacaville, just off Interstate 80 and was a legendary road stop. It first opened in 1921 on the old US Route 40 as a small roadside fruit and nut stand. It grew into a fine restaurant, outdoor eatery, bakery, gift shop, toy shop, and a small railroad that gave rides from the toy shop to the on-site airport. Many celebrities were known to stop to eat and shop at the Nut Tree. All the mothers in our neighborhood loved getting dressed up and driving to the Nut Tree for lunch and shopping.

My first exposure to the ugliness of racism was at the Nut Tree on one of our road trips. We were all dressed up for our visit to San Francisco looking forward to our fancy lunch in Vacaville. We had a

15

beautiful lunch, shopped in the gift store, and then went outside to ride on the giant wooden rocking horses that were lined up on the sidewalk. My sister Anna was two years old. Auntie Nora was holding Anna on her hip while Mom watched and helped the bigger kids. I was about seven years old, and Nora's kids were about five and four.

It was 1962 and everyone was well dressed including Mom and Auntie Nora. A woman came up to Auntie Nora and said, "How sweet that this woman took you in to be her nanny." Mom never missing a beat, charged right up to the woman and said, "Madam, you are very much mistaken. This woman was sweet enough to take me in to be her nanny." The woman looked over and saw Mom holding the hands of Auntie Nora's children. It also didn't hurt that my sister Anna had very black hair and a bit of an almond shape to her eyes.

At the age of seven I knew this was huge, but I was not sure how or why. On the rest of the drive, Mom and Auntie Nora laughed about the "horrid woman." I was not sure if horrid was a good or bad thing. What I was sure of was these two women did not rehash the incident with hatred in their voices. They were hopeful the "horrid woman" had learned something. Auntie Nora went on to earn a Master's Degree in Counselor Education after earning her teaching credential. She continued to be a lifelong educator until her death in October 2007.

# Chapter 2

## K Thru 12th Grade

Every year on the day after Labor Day, the neighborhood moms walked the kids to Fair Oaks Elementary School. It was a big deal and a terrific celebration. It was a rite of passage for the neighborhood kids. My first walk happened when I was three. We were all taking Kurt to kindergarten. The first time I saw the kindergarten room with the tiny toilets and the paint easels, I knew kindergarten was made especially for me. Mrs. Johnson, the teacher, was an added bonus. I cried when we left that day to start our walk home. I wanted to stay in kindergarten with Kurt. When I was four, we all walked Brad to kindergarten and by the time I was five, I was an expert on kindergarten.

I had arrived and life was great! I met kids who, more than fifty years later, are still my closest friends. I learned the pledge of allegiance. I was introduced to musical instruments and learned the words to real songs. I took naps, ate graham crackers and painted pictures using real easels. My mom was proud of everything I said and did at school. I think kindergarten might be the best year of all my twenty plus years of formal education. The rules were simple, and they made sense. Go to school, learn, and have fun.

For the next five years, school was fun and

predictable, except for the second grade. Mrs. Markey, a much older woman and my second grade teacher, was a closeted alcoholic. Her behavior was often unpredictable and irrational. I remember once she locked my classmate Charley inside the giant coat closet. This was his punishment for being disruptive in class. The coat closet also happened to be where the packed lunches were stored.

I sat at my desk feeling terrified that Charley was going to die in that closet. When the recess bell rang, Mrs. Markey did not unlock the coat closet door to let Charley out to play. She left him in there. Out on the playground, I could not get my mind off Charley possibly dying in that closet while we played. By the time we went back inside, it was time to line up for lunch. Mrs. Markey unlocked the door so the kids could get their lunches out of the closet. As she opened the door, Charley walked out with chocolate all over his face. To keep himself occupied and amused while he was locked up, he went through every lunch and ate all the desserts. I remember laughing and thinking to myself Charley was OK.

Mrs. Markey was actively sneaking alcohol during her classroom teaching time, and no one seemed to notice her strange behavior. Years later I asked my mom about all this and she said, "The parents believed she was old and harmless. We agreed to keep an eye on her." Remember there were no alcoholics in Fair Oaks, especially old, second grade teachers.

By sixth grade my world was rapidly changing.

My parents were squabbling a lot and eventually they stopped talking altogether. Mom went to school to get her real estate license and eventually became a broker. Dad enrolled in American River College and later earned an Associate of Arts degree in business. As the oldest child, these changes meant that I grew up fast and assumed responsibilities beyond my years. While my parents may not have meant for their silence to create problems for me, it caused me to try not to rock the boat. This meant that I put their needs and my little sister's needs before my own.

My sister Anna, started kindergarten the first Tuesday after Labor Day in 1965. It was also my first day of sixth grade. By now the neighborhood tradition of everyone walking the kids to school on the first day had long ago been abandoned. Brad and Kurt were attending middle school. Lynn and Kate were in high school, and most of the neighborhood moms were working outside of the home. Auntie Nora, now a high school teacher, had trained her children to walk to school by themselves.

I wanted to make sure Anna had that wonderful first day of kindergarten experience. I walked her to school and showed her the kindergarten classroom. I introduced her to Mrs. Johnson. Anna was shy but excited to begin her new big adventure. I showed her the tiny toilets, the graham crackers, and the musical instruments she would soon learn to play. It was getting time for me to leave. I wanted to get over to the big kids playground and play with my friends

19

before the morning bell rang. As I turned for the door, I saw Anna's bottom lip quiver. I bent down to give her a kiss good-bye, and she leaped into my arms and said "Sissy, please don't leave me." My heart sank because she was not really prepared for this new big adventure. She was more afraid than I had realized. I couldn't leave her there alone in the classroom. I loved this little girl more than anything and never wanted her to feel afraid. That was the beginning of me being Mrs. Johnson's teacher's assistant every day, Monday through Friday for the entire school year.

Every morning before class from that first day to the very last day of Anna's kindergarten, I greeted the students and supervised them on the playground. I helped Anna make friends and watched her grow. During my lunch recess, I would rush back to the kindergarten classroom, pick Anna up and take her to the babysitter's car. I would wave good-bye and then run to the playground to play with my friends.

Graduating from grammar school was hard for me. It was torture knowing I would be leaving Anna behind. Mom was working full time in downtown Sacramento, 16 miles away, and Dad was working full time and attending college. The culture of our family had changed, and our emotional safety was no longer a priority.

The summer after sixth grade was the first time in my life I had ever gone to a babysitter full time. The Thompsons were new to the neighborhood. We didn't really know them well, and we never really did get to know them. The mother, Bev, asked my mom if she could babysit us over the summer. She was a stay at home mom with a baby and needed the money. My parents thought they seemed decent. Mom and Dad hired Bev to be our babysitter for the entire summer. It was awful. They were strange people.

The husband, Rick, had stacks of hardcore pornographic magazines in their den. No one I knew had a den. No one I knew had pornographic magazines. Bev insisted that Anna and I play in the den, and it was ugly and boring in there. We made up games, read books, drew, colored, and talked about everything. The days were very long, and Bev's baby screamed for what seemed like hours. He was always dirty and smelly and sat in the high chair all day long where she could keep her eye on him.

Bev was responsible for making us lunch, and every day she made Kraft Macaroni and Cheese from the blue box. For good measure, she threw in a piece of bologna once in a while or a can of tuna. There were no snacks passed out throughout the day because Bev said "Our parents did not pay her enough."

Daily by about 3:00 p.m., Anna who was six years old would complain about being hungry. Bev would not let us play outside. She said it was too dangerous, and she would be held responsible if we got hurt. Her house was unbelievably hot and never smelled good. Every afternoon I told Bev I needed to go home and get something. After a lot of begging, she eventually let me go to our house.

I could not wait to escape the clutches of Bev. I would bust open the front door and run down the street, open our garage door and sit with our dog Blondie crying, "I want my mom. I want my mom." Then I would pick myself up, go inside the house to our kitchen and grab a handful of Cheerios to take back to my sister so she could have a snack.

My parents were not being cruel or neglectful. They were being tricked. Every time they arrived to pick us up, Bev had showered, cleaned up her baby, and cleaned the filthy kitchen. She turned on the air conditioner that was in the living room window, started cooking dinner, and had us sitting quietly on her couch waiting for our parents to arrive.

I would try and tell my parents how awful it was at the Thompson house, but I never mentioned the magazines, heat, filth, or lack of food. Even though Rick never touched us, he talked to us in a creepy manner, and I was afraid of him. Because of the cryptic way I tried to communicate with my parents, I believe they thought I was a moody pre-teen who didn't want a babysitter. By 1967 when I started seventh grade, the Thompson's had divorced, sold their home, and Bev moved out of state because her husband got into some trouble.

The Felix family bought the Thompson home and ended up being terrific neighbors. Mr. Felix was a Highway Patrol Officer, and Mrs. Felix was expecting their first child and coincidentally was looking for a babysitting job. Auntie Nora and Mom both needed after school childcare. This time they thoroughly interviewed Mrs. Felix and after feeling more than satisfied, hired her to watch all the little kids.

I convinced my parents to let me stay at home alone. I was, after all, in the seventh grade. Anna and Auntie Nora's children loved Mrs. Felix and loved going to her house. They got to play, do arts and crafts, and got fun snacks. This time the house was clean, bright, and cheerful, and Mrs. Felix was a wonderful woman and neighbor.

The year of my seventh grade, Mom lost nearly 80 pounds. She was working full time, buying new clothes, and feeling beautiful at the young age of 34. She was successful in her real estate career. Her self-esteem was on the rise, and she was feeling good about herself and the future of our family. However, things did not get better with our family. Years later Mom told me, "I never felt pretty enough for your Dad. I thought if I lost weight and got cuter, he would love me more, but he didn't." I could feel the pain in her heart.

I do not know the ins and outs of what went on in my mom and dad's marriage. Over the years I have heard a lot of "he saids" and "she saids." I am sure the truth is evenly split somewhere in the middle. The bottom line is their marriage did not survive. They both were wounded and not able to communicate with one another at any level. Their problems grew until they broke the family apart for good.

It would be six years before my parents' divorce would become final. For six long years I would get glimmers of hope that my family would get back together. Those six years were hell on me, Anna, and my parents. One week they hated each other, and the next week they loved each other. I was in a state of confusion all the time, and my nerves were always on edge. My stomach would burn. Some nights I was unable to sleep, and some days I slept all day.

Everything in my life was changing and not for the better. I missed my family, I missed my parents, and I missed my life as I had known it. My heart felt like it had a huge hole in it. Nothing was going good for me, and I felt alone, unimportant, and invisible. Everyone seemed to be busy, and no one had time to check in on one another. My parents were going in opposite directions. Our home was filled with pain. It was sad and I was sad.

During my high school years, I began sneaking food and hiding it in my bedroom closet, mostly candy. At our local grocery store, H&H Market, I charged two full boxes of licorice, one red and one black. Each box had 500 pieces inside and cost five dollars. That was a lot of money back then, especially for candy. H&H Market had a special set up for locals who were faithful customers. Basically, it was a card box that had file cards inside with the family names written along the top of the card. Just below the name, the grocer would mark down the items purchased and the total cost of the purchases. Then customers would sign their names, and at a later date would stop in and pay their bills.

My dad never liked charging anything. He preferred to pay cash. It was my mom who charged the groceries. On a particular Saturday, I was at the H&H Market with my dad, when the owner said, "Hey Stan, you want to pay your bill today?" My dad laughed and said, "Sure." The owner pulled out the file card with our name on it, and the total included my $10 charge for my candy. Right there on the card was my signature next to the licorice purchase. I could see my dad was upset. He looked at me sternly and quietly said, "What's this?" I was so embarrassed, and in a small voice I said, "Candy."

Neither one of us ever mentioned this uncomfortable incident again. Even to this day, the fact that we had no discussion about my behavior makes me quite sad. We were definitely a no talk family, and when things got too emotional, we went silent. Instead of talking though my feelings, I became the girl who drowned them out with a box of candy. When my emotions became overwhelming and too difficult to manage, I ate candy and then felt calm. This was and still is a hard habit to break.

# Chapter 3

# College Years

January 1974, I graduated mid-term from high school. During the graduation ceremony I gave a speech entitled, "Why Advance To Reality?" My high school years were tough, and I knew I wasn't the only student on campus who had struggled emotionally. Many of us needed to grab on to some hope that our futures could be better than our lives during the high school years. My speech was written to create hope for that better future. I couldn't wait to go to college and get started with what I believed was going to be a better life.

I knew my next phase was going to be wonderful. I always knew I would go to college. While growing up my mom never said "If you go to college," she only said, "When you go to college." Going to college was a given. Communication and sharing emotions were never a strong part of our family, even during good times. Each of my family members were hurting. We were a united front of trying to hold ourselves together, at least to the public.

My family had the only parents on our street who were getting a divorce (other than the horrible Thompson family). At age 17 the pain was terrible. The humiliation and embarrassment were unbearable. I felt like we were being judged. I felt lonely and alone. I went to college as fast as I could to make life good again for me and my family. I believed if I would have been prettier, skinnier, or better behaved as a teenager, my parents would not be divorcing. Maybe if I went to college and got a degree, my parents would get back together, and all would be good again. I held onto that impossible dream for as long as I could.

After my high school graduation, Mom moved into a fancy new Fair Oaks apartment complex. Her new apartment was gorgeous. She seemed relaxed and happy there. Even though she appeared to be happy, I wanted her to move back home. By early May, Mom and I were not getting along at all. I was furious because she would not move home, and she was furious because I was taking sides and butting into her marriage and divorce.

Later in May, without warning, Mom walked into our family home and said, "Stan, I want to let you know, I am moving into this house and you are moving out. This move is happening on Saturday so make some plans for you and Julie." Dad, Anna, and I just stood there looking at her. Our world was about to change drastically again.

On Saturday, Dad and I moved into one of his rental homes a few miles away in Carmichael. Mom made it clear I needed to move with Dad and Anna was to stay with her. It killed me to leave Anna behind, I had become her second mother The day we moved was one of the hardest days of my life. Lots of tears were shed. Our family was clearly broken up for good.

By age 19, I was still enrolled and attending American River College (ARC). I use the word attending lightly. I was enrolled at ARC and attended my classes sometimes. Everything seemed hard. Life was hard. Family was hard. Work was hard, and school was even harder. I had been on and off academic probation the entire time I attended ARC.

College for me was easy, fun, and hard all at the same time. I am an auditory learner, but at the time I did not know there were different ways to learn. I did know I loved hearing the lectures, thinking about what the instructors were saying, and participating in the discussion groups. I learned best by listening. Taking multiple choice tests that determined my entire grade became disastrous.

I almost always flunked the exams. Most of my grades were either an A or a F. I remember on many occasions crying to myself saying, "I know the answer. I wish I could just tell them." All the written answers looked the same to me. I was told to eliminate the most obvious wrong answer. Unfortunately for me, I could never figure out which one that was.

You might be wondering how I got any good grades at all. If the instructor added other assignments to our grades such as papers or projects, I aced them. Eventually going to class began to intimidate me. I was afraid the instructor would call on me, and I did not feel very smart. However, I loved learning.

One day I was walking past a large lecture hall on campus. I went in and grabbed a theater style seat. It was cool and dark in the hall. The instructor was teaching a class on Political Science. I was fascinated and started taking notes in my notebook. I came back for every class until the semester ended. I moved from the back of the room to the front row. The teacher asked my name and remembered it. I don't think he realized I was not technically enrolled in his class. It was a relief to know my learning style would never be judged by a test score. I sat in on several lecture style classes over the next few semesters. This was an excellent way for me to learn. Since I was not enrolled in any of these classes, my grade point average (GPA) was not looking good at all. In other words, I was flunking out of college.

In the late spring of 1975, I figured it was time for me to get a job. I applied for and got an on-call position as a custodian for Sacramento County General Services. My hope was to start there and move into another area of county employment when I graduated from college. As a backup plan, since college was not going well, maybe I could get a permanent position as a custodian. Either way, it was a place to start the government career I wanted.

Being an on-call custodian was the perfect job for me. The hours were 5:00 p.m. to 1:00 a.m. If I wanted to work I called in, and if I did not want to work, I did not call in. The pay was amazing, and we got paid for two breaks of fifteen minutes each and a thirty minute lunch period. It felt great having money in my pocket. For the first time, I was starting to feel like a real grown up person. My self-esteem and confidence were on the rise. With a renewed interest in college, I actually worked my way off academic probation. I was revved up and ready to go. The spring semester was ending, soon, and my plan was to hit the ground running in September for the fall semester.

During the summer, I wanted to work and earn as much money as I could. I wanted to build up my savings account. I planned to read books from the library on how to properly take tests. About three weeks into June, my boss asked if I would be willing to work at the downtown location. So far, I had only cleaned buildings at the corporation yard. The buildings I cleaned included Refuse, Juvenile Hall, Social Services, Animal Control, and a few other buildings. We would meet at the office at 5:00 p.m. when we'd be assigned our buildings, and we left in our own cars to the various locations. At 12:30 a.m. we would return to the office, check out, and leave. It was great! I worked alone, talking only with employees who were in the buildings where I cleaned. I had my radio and my paperback book. It was a perfect situation for a shy girl with very low self-esteem and hardly any confidence. Alone time was what I craved.

My boss kept asking me if I would be willing to work downtown. Against my better judgment, I agreed to go to the Sacramento Courthouse for one week. One of the guys was on vacation, and they needed a substitute. My first day at the courthouse, I arrived early, around 4:30 p.m. because I wanted to make a good first impression.

I was totally overwhelmed when I first walked through the door. Loud music was playing, and about 15 guys were sitting around talking, laughing, reading the paper, and playing poker and dominoes. I almost turned and ran for the closest exit. This would have been difficult since the office was located in the basement. I was about to inch my way towards the elevator when the downtown supervisor, Joe, figured I was leaving and motioned for me to approach his giant desk. I was glad he did because after he introduced me to the guys, I felt very welcomed.

When I agreed to this arrangement, I did not know that I was one of only four female custodians working for the county. In addition to that, I did not know I was the youngest employee in this entire department. By the time my week was over, we all had become fast friends, and all the guys were very helpful. After that week, I returned to working at the corporation yard. This location was my favorite. I liked the quiet, and I loved working alone.

About a month later in July 1975, my boss got a request from the downtown supervisor, Joe, who said some of the guys were going on vacation and were requesting me to be their substitute. You see each guy had what was called "his run." That means they were responsible to keep their areas of the courthouse clean.

Some substitute custodians merely cleaned the surfaces, but I really cleaned. There is nothing worse than coming back from a vacation and having your run be filthy.

This time when I showed up to the office downtown, I was not shy or afraid. I walked in with confidence, and the guys greeted me warmly. A young guy, Jimmy Jenkins, was there. He was about a year older than me. I had not seen him before. I guess it was his run I cleaned the first time I was assigned to this post. He took a rather aggressive interest in me. I was not used to being around flirty guys, and his behavior made me very nervous and uncomfortable. I mostly tried to ignore him, but he was pretty aggressive throughout the night. I couldn't wait for the shift to be over so I could go home. Unfortunately, I had committed to this assignment for two weeks. He kept asking me out, and I kept telling him no thank you. Then one night after he asked me out, and I refused once again. He aggressively said, "Why? Do you think you are too good for me?" He had hit my weak spot. Of course I did not think I was too good for him. I did not feel good enough for anyone. I was shy, and my self-esteem was low. I was barely escaping flunking out of college, and my confidence was nearly nonexistent. I did not say those words out loud, but I did say them loud and clear to myself, and then I told him yes, we could go out.

I did not date much in high school. But from what little I did know about dates, I was expecting him to set a time, pick a place, get dressed up, pick me up, and pay the dinner tab. After I said yes, he asked for my phone number. When he called to set things up, he explained he did not have a car, had no driver license, did not know how to read, did not like to go to fancy restaurants because he was under age and liked beer, and lived in Roseville, about 12 miles from my house. This information was already giving me a really bad headache. I tried several times to beg my way out. Always the people pleaser, I kept trying to politely get myself out of this mess. But he kept beating me at my own game. Finally, I convinced myself it was easier to go out with him once and then be done with him. That was easier said than done. He was fresh in from Tennessee, had no friends his age in California, and needed transportation to do some fun things.

I picked him up on Irene Street in Roseville. He shared a cute little yellow house with an older co-worker. It was a two bedroom, one bath house decorated modestly and was very clean. He jumped into my 1963 white Volkswagen Bug, and away we went to the nearest McDonalds. He got the food to go, so we could picnic at Folsom Lake. As he talked, I realized we had even less in common than I thought on the phone. He was raised in the mountains of Tennessee and only went to school until the third grade. He was one of 14 kids and never learned to read. His father was a retired refrigeration guy who drank like a fish. His brothers had been in and out of prison for years. Some of his siblings were products

33

of affairs and other marriages.

My head was spinning with all his family information. I really didn't care for this guy and couldn't wait to go home. Are you seeing a pattern here? I did not like this guy, but I did not have the personal skills to get rid of him. My words were not matching my behavior; therefore, he did not believe what I was telling him. As I was leaving, hoping to never see him again, I think he could feel me slipping away. Then he said, "Would you teach me to read?" Oh no, he found another weak spot. I always needed to be helpful. I said "OK." Our tutoring sessions took place at his house because he had no car and could not drive anywhere. After about a month, we started to become friendly. He began sharing about his childhood and background. I was curious because it was so very different from how I was raised. We started comparing notes, and then after tutoring he would invite me to sit out back and talk while we drank iced tea. He would sing old hillbilly ballads and pick me lilacs from the lilac tree in the yard. I started seeing a gentler and kinder side of Jimmy. Eventually he bought some nice clothes, took and passed his driver license test, and got a car.

I was living with my dad in Carmichael, at this time. One day in mid-August 1975, I came home and found my dad sitting at the kitchen table looking over a bunch of papers. He looked up as I walked in and said, "Hey, I sold the duplex." We were living together on a piece of property my dad owned. It had two houses that were connected together by a carport. This was temporary housing for us while we built a house on Fair Oaks Boulevard. My dad, sister, and I were all going to live in the new house upon completion. I said to my dad, "But the house isn't ready." He said, "Yes, I know. Do you have a place where you can go live for a while?" He was moving in with his girlfriend down the street and the Fair Oaks Boulevard house was going to be rented to their friends upon completion. I was stunned. I had plans. I was going to rededicate myself in college and going to graduate and get a better job. I was just catching a firm sense of my own stability. Now what? I told him that I did have a place to move when in reality I did not have anywhere to go.

The next time I went to Roseville, Jimmy and his roommate insisted that I would be living with them. I was devastated and felt totally abandoned by my dad. Feeling trapped by circumstances beyond my control, I couldn't come up with a better solution than to move in with Jimmy for a few weeks until I could find an apartment of my own. Unfortunately, it was a disastrous decision on my part because, within months I would be married to a man I did not respect and did not love.

# Chapter 4

# The Marriage

When the summer of 1975 came to an end I moved out of Jimmy's house. I was again hopeful for a fresh start. Historically, new school years filled me with a spirit of new beginnings, and this year was no different. I was again determined to come up with a new plan. This time I would make a plan that would get me out of this dating and housing mess.

In addition to the on-call custodian job, I was working as a dishwasher at the Le Normande restaurant in Carmichael. Mom's Greek friend Alex was the owner, and she was his hostess. Working together helped us strengthen our mother-daughter relationship. I worked the dinner shift which allowed me to attend college during the day. The waiters shared their tips with me because they loved my mom. The guys grew to love me and started treating me like a kid sister. The chef fed me at work and gave me leftovers each night. This helped keep my food bill down.

My earnings, combined with savings from my county employment, allowed me to secure a furnished studio apartment for myself. The apartment was located conveniently on the border of Fair Oaks and Carmichael. Anna, who was now 14 years old, would come stay with me often. When I moved out of Jimmy's in Roseville and into my own apartment, I believed I was on my way to freedom.

I did not have the much needed support or knowledge to come up with an adequate plan to escape the clutches of Jimmy. Because of this, my plan turned into "wishing he would go away." One Friday morning in September my wish came true. Jimmy had decided to return to Tennessee permanently. He realized things were not working out between us and was going home. He said he needed one last favor. He already had his bus ticket and just needed a ride to the bus station. He had a very early morning departure. That was one favor I gladly agreed to.

The moment I saw the bus leave the station, I felt total relief. Finally my wish had come true. I was free of Jimmy for good, and 2,554 miles were going to separate us.

My life was finally back to feeling normal. I mentioned my apartment came furnished. There was a corner unit bed set. It had two twin beds that pushed up under a corner table. During the day it was a couch, and at night it was two twin beds. Mom was working two full time jobs by then, and Dad was working and dating Jacky. Anna loved coming to my apartment and staying the night. It was close enough that she could ride over on her bike. Anna was there so often I had a key made for her. I loved it when I came home and found her sitting at my kitchen table doing her homework. She'd call Mom at Le Normande to get permission to have a sleepover at my place. We were all getting very close again. Life finally seemed good.

In 1975, the easiest place for a young woman to get birth control pills was at Planned Parenthood in Sacramento. In those days driving to downtown Sacramento was a bit of a trek and took some planning. My birth control pills ran out in early September. If you were under 21, they only gave one three-month supply at a time. Every three months you were required to talk with a doctor and explain why you still needed "The Pill." I hated this process but followed their procedures so I would not get pregnant.

The birth control pill holders held 21 pills. You were on the pill for three weeks, then off for a week. The week Jimmy left was my week off the pill. I did not have a follow-up appointment with Planned Parenthood to refill my order. I decided to quit taking the pills. At that time, there was great concern surrounding the safety of birth control pills. Jimmy was gone, and I was not dating anyone. I craved a calm, quiet, and uncomplicated life. My goal was to enjoy my family and finish college. Therefore, I did not need the pills.

On Saturday night October 4th, I came home from Le Normande around 1:00 a.m. As I walked up the sidewalk, I noticed my drapes were open and the TV was playing. A big smile came to my face. I was excited because Anna was there to surprise me. I ran up the stairs, threw open the door and saw Jimmy sitting there in the glow of the television light.

Budweiser beer cans and bottles were everywhere. I turned to run, and he grabbed me and dragged me into the apartment. I raced for the telephone, and he pulled the cord out of the wall. I asked how he had got into my apartment, and he said the office woman was most helpful. Jimmy could be very charming when he tried, and he had convinced her that I wanted him there.

Feeling trapped, alone, and vulnerable in the middle of the night was one of the most frightening experiences I've ever had. No one was available to help me, and all my escape plans had failed. He started undressing and demanding sex. I told him no and explained I was no longer on the pill. Jimmy said that was the best news he had heard all month. He refused to take no for an answer insisting, "We need to make a son!" I begged him to leave or at the very least to leave me alone. He did neither. He insisted on having sex, and when he was done, he said, "Baby, we just made ourselves a son." Then he went back to the chair and drank all the beer he had left.

I was in shock and felt completely numb. I did not come out of it for weeks. Jimmy refused to leave my apartment. The office lady really liked him, flirted with him, and refused to help me kick him out. I called the sheriff to have Jimmy removed. When the sheriff finally arrived he spoke to me, Jimmy and the office lady. He made a few notes on his clipboard and then said, "One of you needs to move out and you need to decide who it will be." Since my name was the only name on the rental agreement I said, "He needs to move out." The sheriff looked at both of us and said, "I don't want to get involved with two 19 year olds playing house." At that time, law enforcement tried not to intervene in domestic squabbles, and the laws around date and marital rape were not commonly being enforced. Jimmy was so convincing when he lied, and I was so used to being silent when things were uncomfortable that I wasn't able to make the sheriff understand how bad my situation was.

I continued to work at Le Normande. For six weeks I waited for my period to start. In those days, a woman had to wait six weeks for a pregnancy test. By week four I was pretty sure I was pregnant. November 17th I was finally eligible for the test. It was just a week before Thanksgiving. After the test you have to wait a few days before you could call in to obtain the results. I called in and got the news that I was indeed pregnant, and the baby was due July 4, 1976. Jimmy anxiously awaited the results and jumped for joy when I told him I was pregnant.

The next week I went to my Godmother Thelma Wolf's house to tell her I was pregnant. She had helped two other girls through their pregnancies. I felt safest telling her first. I knew I was not staying with Jimmy. I also knew I wanted my baby and was going to raise him alone.

Thelma and I sat down at her kitchen table, and I

gave her the news. She was not pleased, but she did not seem surprised. The first sentence out of her mouth was, "OK, let's set the date for you to get married." I quietly told her that I did not want to get married. She asked me what the father wanted, and I told her he wanted marriage. At that point she pulled out her calendar. She picked a date in January when her husband was not working at Weinstock's department store. Then she told me we were going to dress shop with my Godfather's employee discount.

Everything started moving quickly. She had most of the details settled before I told my parents the pregnancy news. My Godmother always had my best interest in her heart, but she was from a different generation. According to her, "When a young girl got pregnant she got married." I was insecure and passive and did not stand up for myself. The wedding was set for the evening of January 23, 1976 at the Fair Oaks Community Clubhouse.

Thelma and I went to Weinstock's the next week and found a pretty white wedding dress that fit me perfectly. It was on sale for $125, and with the employee discount she paid $93.75 plus tax. We bought the dress in November for a wedding in January that was to be worn by a pregnant bride. Amazingly, it still fit me at the wedding.

I had no desire to plan a wedding. I could not stand Jimmy and still innocently believed I could get out of this mess. My family and friends were getting worried and began offering to bring food for the reception. My wedding turned into a potluck dinner. The centerpieces were camellias from my best friend Cindy's yard. Jimmy wore a brown suit he purchased at Kmart.

The day of the wedding, Cindy and I were alone in the hall as we hung borrowed folding pink and white bells on the walls. She looked at me and said, "What the fuck are you doing?" I said, "I have no idea." Cindy said, "Let's go to Tahoe right now. You don't have to do this." We looked at each other, set our bells down and walked across the park and got hamburgers, fries, and milkshakes at the drive-in. After eating, we went back and finished decorating the hall with the 20 fold up bells.

My family gathered at the family home to get ready for the wedding. We were having so much fun just being together. I did not want to leave. It certainly did not help that I hated the idea of getting married to Jimmy. I was in the bathtub at the exact time my wedding was supposed to start. It was nearly 8:00 p.m. by the time I arrived at the clubhouse where the wedding and reception were to take place. It felt like I was going to the guillotine.

# Chapter 5

# The Escape

I now have a complete understanding why people do not "just leave" when they are living in a violent situation. Jimmy was extremely violent during our marriage. His behavior included yelling, hitting, slapping, biting, shoving, putting holes in the wall, throwing things, cheating with other women, isolating me from my friends and family, and intimidating me with threats of future violence if I even thought about leaving. The only thing predictable in my marriage was the violence was never going to stop.

My real education regarding escaping violence began during the Thanksgiving weekend in 1978, when I had had enough! I wanted away from all the crazy and dangerous domestic violence in my life. My son, Jeffrey, was almost two and a half years old and a total joy to be around. Thank goodness he was a happy baby because we were isolated from family. There were no neighbors living close, and friends quit stopping by.

It was Saturday night on this particular Thanksgiving weekend when my life was totally turned upside down. The weather was cold, and it was pouring down rain. Jimmy left with his brother, Lawrence, to go to a bar in downtown Sacramento.

According to his brother, Jimmy would not stop ordering beers and got more drunk than usual. Lawrence said he tried to encourage Jimmy to leave the bar, but he refused. One of our old coworkers from Sacramento County General Services walked into the bar. Throughout our marriage, Jimmy had accused me of having affairs with anyone and everyone. Now he was drunk and accused our coworker John of sleeping with me. John denied the allegations and encouraged Jimmy to go home to his wife and son.

Jimmy hated being told what to do, especially by someone he thought was sleeping with his wife. He called John some horrible names and made more nasty accusations. John ignored him and went back to drinking his beer.

Lawrence was still trying to get Jimmy out of the bar. He wanted to get Jimmy back out to Fair Oaks, and then be on his own way home. Jimmy was very drunk, and very angry, and he turned and hit his brother in the jaw. Lawrence got mad and left, leaving Jimmy to find his own way home.

Jimmy called me, but he did not ask for a ride home. He asked me to join him at the bar. I should have been more suspicious. He never invited me out. I did not drink, and I hated hanging out in bars. Furthermore, I had my son, and I was painting his bedroom. I didn't want to take Jeffrey out in the rain. Nothing felt good about this phone call. He begged me and pressured me in the exact way he did when we first met.

It was awful. He was not accepting no for an answer. He was pushy, demanding, threatening, and controlling. Then he said, "I'd like to have an evening out with my wife." The bottom fell out of my stomach. With my nerves on edge, I regrettably agreed to meet him at the downtown bar.

I washed the paint out of my hair, put on some clean clothes, and packed up little Jeffrey. Jimmy's sister, Barbara, agreed to babysit but she insisted on keeping our son overnight so she could go to bed and sleep without being disturbed.

I hated bars and walking into a bar alone on a Saturday night after 11:00 p.m. was my idea of hell on earth. I stood in the doorway, adjusting to the darkness, the smoke, and the loud music. I was wishing the earth would swallow me up. Before that happened, I saw Jimmy at the far end of the bar. He waved for me to come down to where he was standing. I nearly ran the length of the room looking down at my feet. I sat down on the bar stool closest to the wall. The bartender asked me what I wanted to drink, and I ordered ice water. Money was tight, and besides I never drank. I think the bartender was relieved and hoped I would get Jimmy out as soon as possible.

The bartender set my water down. I was about to take a sip when Jimmy said, "Hey, your boyfriend is here." He had an evil sneer on his face. I am sure I looked confused. Not only did I not have a boyfriend, I had hardly any friends at all. No one wanted to hang around while this crazy-acting man was in my life.

Jimmy was standing in front of the bar. He stepped back, and on the very next stool was my old coworker John. I started to smile and get excited about seeing an old friend. All those guys had been so nice to me. They were instrumental in building my self-confidence and self-esteem when it was pretty low. John did not greet me warmly, but instead gave me a clear nonverbal message to say nothing. He was an older man and much wiser in the ways of the world than I was. I gave him a soft hello and looked back at my glass of water with the twist of lemon.

I sat there wondering how my life had gotten to such a low point. I knew it was time, even past time, to get out of this marriage. I was quietly planning my future escape. I wasn't really paying attention to what Jimmy was saying until I heard him spouting off words about me that were lies. Then it hit me. This is a set up! I started really listening to what Jimmy was saying to everyone in the bar. He was egging John on, but John was ignoring him. Jimmy's temper was growing, and he was getting more agitated by the minute. He was getting ready to explode. I had seen it many times. I knew his cycle of violence all too well. My stomach was starting to hurt. I could barely breathe, and was looking frantically for a safe escape route for myself. I was starting to shake and thought I was going to faint. Then I wished I would faint, so they would call an ambulance. I was having my first panic attack, and I did not know what to do. I could not

46

find my voice. The words were simple. I needed to look at the bartender and say, "Please help me." But the words would not come.

Just when I thought things could not get any worse, Jimmy knocked John's hat off his head and socked him in the jaw. Within minutes, a bar fight had erupted between Jimmy and John. Fists were flying, tables were being knocked over, and drinks were being spilled. The patrons broke up the fight, and the bartender kicked us out of the bar. John begged me to stay, and Jimmy demanded that I leave. I still could not find my voice to utter three simple words, "Please help me."

I had driven Jimmy's work car down to the bar since he had long ago wrecked my Volkswagen Bug. The work car was a 1962 Valiant station wagon we called "The Frog" because of the shape of the front end. He kept his wooden toolbox full of tools in the back. Jimmy was so drunk he could not walk, so luckily he told me to drive. He demanded we go get Jeffrey. I explained Barbara was keeping him overnight. Jimmy yelled, "That's my boy, and we're getting him tonight." It was now nearly 1:00 a.m. We were riding down a quiet street in East Sacramento, and Jimmy's behaviors and words were escalating again. I am not exactly sure what he was saying, because I was trying to figure out a way to escape this violent man before he went off on me.

Then I heard the words that scared the hell out of me and changed my life forever. He said, "People have to hit you to get you to hear them. I know you think you are leaving but you're not. I don't want another man raising my son. I will take us out before I let that happen." Then he grabbed the hair at the back of my head and started pounding on my face. My nose was bleeding. My lips were cut. My teeth felt loose, and my eyes were closing up. He reached into the back and grabbed a hammer out of his toolbox and raised it over his head to strike me. I thought to myself, "Oh my God! He is going to kill me!"

I needed a plan, and I needed one fast. Then it came to me. I had seen it on television a hundred times. I would speed up the car, jump out, and the car would crash into a telephone pole. Then the car would blow up. He would die, and I would be free forever. It was a perfect plan in theory. I sped up the car and jumped out. When I hit the ground, my body went flying. My clog shoes went in opposite directions, my pants ripped, and my ankle was badly sprained.

It was all worth it, or so I thought. The car did not crash because Jimmy temporarily sobered up rather quickly and steered it to safety. I knew I had a minute or maybe seconds to get help. It was very dark on the street. Then I saw a cute little well-cared-for home with a porch light shining bright. I raced for that porch and frantically rang the doorbell. I banged on the solid door until an older man answered. I could see his face through the locked screen door. He looked so kind, and right then I found my voice,

"Please help me." He reached over to open the locked screen door, and I felt relief.

My hope was soaring. I started to relax, and for the first time in what seemed like forever I was feeling a little safe. Then before he opened the screen door, he slammed his big solid wooden door shut and turned the lock. I looked over my shoulder, and Jimmy was standing there with a crazed look on his face. My heart sank. He grabbed me by the back of my pants, and he started dragging me back to the street.

By now the rain had stopped. The air was clean, and the stars were brightly shining. He stopped us on the sidewalk and hugged me so tightly the air was forced out of my lungs. Then he said, "I love you more than anyone will ever love you. Why don't you know that?" I looked up and stared at those bright stars and mouthed these words to God, "Please help me."

I encouraged Jimmy to keep hugging me because on the street I felt safer than getting back into that car. I was facing the west looking over Jimmy's shoulder and wondering if this was going to be my last night on earth. I had no more tricks up my sleeve. As the tears started to fall from my eyes, I looked out and saw two Sacramento city police cars turning the corner. One was coming from the north and one from the south.

The first police car pulled up to the curb right next to us. The officer rolled down his window but didn't get out. Jimmy was explaining and convincing the officer that we were married, and we had a small tiff, and things were good now. The officer was believing this story and was getting ready to leave. Jimmy still had his arm around me and was holding me very tight, so tight in fact I could hardly breathe. It was his way of warning me that I had better not say one word to these police officers.

Minutes ago I had found my voice and asked for help, but the words were not coming now when I needed them the most. I knew if these officers left I would probably die, so I reached my hand into the open police car window and grabbed the officer's leg. He started to move his leg, and I grabbed tighter. It was the only way I could think of to get my message out, "Please help me."

The officer sat there silently not saying a word. We stared at each other for the longest time. Finally, he opened his car door and stepped out. The second officer was parked directly behind the first police car. He was sitting there doing paperwork. When he looked up and saw the other officer stepping out of his car and saw Jimmy getting agitated, he jumped out of his car.

The officers huddled together and decided to split us up and speak to us separately. Before this could happen, Jimmy went ballistic. He started yelling at me, "What did you do? What did you do? You stupid bitch. What did you do?" Then he began socking me in the face and ribs. The second officer threw Jimmy on the ground, put the handcuffs on him, and threw him in the back of his police car.

Under the dimness of the street lights, the officers assessed the damage to my face. They encouraged me to go to an emergency room. I made it clear I wanted to get my young son and go to my mom's house out in Fair Oaks. They agreed to my plan if I promised to go straight to my mom's after I picked up Jeffrey. They had their dispatch people call Barbara and tell her to have Jeffrey packed and ready to go when I got there. By now it was past 2:00 a.m. They checked out the car to make sure it was drivable and told me to get my son and get over to my mom's as quickly as possible. They assured me Jimmy would be in jail for a long time.

When I picked up Jeffrey, Barbara was very worried about her younger brother and wanted details. I told her to call the jail, and they could give her all the details she needed. I left that night hoping to never see anyone from that family ever again. For the first time in a very long time I felt empowered, confident, and proud that I had found my voice. I was escaping, and life was going to be good again.

About 30 minutes later I was ringing my mom's doorbell. It was nearly 3:00 am. Jeffrey was wide awake and in his usual great mood. I could hear Mom on the other side of the door saying, "Who is it?" "It's me Mom, Julie." She was not yet married to Dennis, but he was living in her home. Anna, still in high school, was sound asleep.

Mom opened the door, took one look at my bruised and bloodied face and started crying

51

hysterically. Then she started chanting, "Oh my God. Oh my God. Oh my God." Then she started yelling, "I am going to kill that bastard. I am going to kill that bastard!" Dennis took one look at me and drew me into his arms and gave me the biggest, best hug I had ever received in my entire life. He rocked me and said, "Everything is going to be all right."

We were all standing on the porch when Jeffrey came out from behind my leg and said in his cute little beautiful always cheerful voice, "Yia Yia, why are you crying?" We all looked at this little two and a half year old and started laughing. I was home, and I knew life was going to be good again.

Dennis told Mom to go and get me cleaned up. We stepped into the front bathroom of my family home, and that was the first time I saw my mangled and bloodied face. It was the first time I realized for sure my teeth really were loose. Mom assured me they would tighten back up if I was careful with them. She cleaned me up, gave me one of her nightgowns, made me hot tea, had me take two aspirins, then put me to bed in my old room.

Jeffrey and I shared a queen size bed that night. After he was finally back to sleep, I lay there thinking about my future. I had asked for help and had finally escaped my violent situation. There were no more secrets, and my family was on my team. With peace in my heart, I started to drift off to sleep. Within a few minutes, my entire bedroom was brightened up by car headlights. I jumped up and looked out the window. I saw a car half in the road and half on the grass. The headlights were pointing right at my bedroom window. Jimmy jumped out of his sister's car yelling, "Julie, I know you're in there. You had better get out here right now with my boy."

It had only been three hours since the police had taken him to jail "for a very long time." How could this be happening? I ran down the hall yelling, "He's here. He's here." By this time, he was trying to break down the front door with a crow bar. Dennis opened the door and tried to reason with him. Jimmy exploded, breaking things and hitting everyone and everything that got in his way. I locked the bedroom door where Jeffrey was sleeping, hoping he would not wake up.

Jimmy was furious with Mom, yelling she was interfering with his family. He was pushing his way down the hall trying to get to my mom. As Jimmy and Dennis were fighting, they bumped up against Anna's closed bedroom door. She must have sensed danger because she came out of her room holding her baseball bat. She quickly assessed the situation and started beating the crap out of Jimmy. He was unstoppable and kept plowing his way down the hall trying to get to Mom.

I ran out the front door over to Uncle Ed's house asking for help and to use their phone. Uncle Ed ran next door to help, and I called the Sheriff. Three Sheriff's cars arrived within minutes. Again, he was cuffed and put in the back of the patrol car. I was again assured, "He will be in jail for a very long time." His sister's car was hauled away by a tow truck.

By 8:00 a.m. the next morning Jimmy, who had walked from our house to Mom's house, was standing on the front porch ringing the doorbell. He apologized to Mom and Dennis and assured everyone he was so sorry, and this would never happen again. None of us believed him, and I had no intentions of ever living with this man again. Then he said he would leave for good if I would listen to what he had to say out on the porch. My mom was leery, but thought I would be safe if I did not leave the porch, and we left the front door open. We stepped outside, and with a smile on his face, he said, "If you and my boy don't get home immediately, I will find a way to kill them all. You have one hour to say your good-byes and get home." Then he turned, walked to his work car, got in, and left.

I was shaken to the core of my very being. I was really scared for my family. No one, not even law enforcement was able to stop him. No one was going to be able to keep me safe. I went inside and told my mom I was going home and would be needing a ride. Mom and Dennis asked me to please stay. I could tell they were beyond worried. I now believed they needed protection from this beast who was in our family because of me. If he was going to hit and hurt anyone, it needed to be me, not my entire family. When my hour was up, I asked for a ride and Dennis took me home. He hugged me good-bye, then made me promise to call if Jimmy got violent with me again. We both had tears in our eyes as he drove away.

Every day Mom came to my house or I went to her house. She was very protective of me and Jeffrey. Mom was Jimmy's boss at A.G. Spanos' property development company. She kept a close eye on him at work. Mom was relentless with keeping us safe. She made it very clear to Jimmy that she was watching his every move, and that not one hair on her daughter's head better ever be harmed again. He hated the situation, and he was growing to hate Mom.

Life was calm for the next week or so. Jimmy worked Tuesdays through Saturdays. The first Saturday in December he came home for lunch like he did every day. Lunch was ready for him, but Jeffrey and I were not there. We had gone over to my Mom's house for a visit. Jimmy was furious and drove over to Mom's home and barged in when Mom opened the front door. Mom told him to calm down and to get back to work. He argued with her. But she stood firm. He stormed off.

Jimmy drove over to my dad's house. He told my dad and his wife Jacky there was a serious matter that needed to be discussed. He explained we were all moving to Tennessee to get some "breathing space" from my mother. He further explained my mom had too much "dysfunctional influence" over me. I don't really know what else they talked about. What I do know is Jimmy asked my dad for a large loan to cover moving expenses, and my dad, thinking he was helping me, wrote him out a check.

# Chapter 6

## The Kidnapping

After Jimmy left my dad's house, he drove directly over to my mom's house. He ordered me to "get the baby and to get my ass home." I told him no. I wasn't leaving, and I wasn't going to live with him any longer. He was furious with me because I wasn't letting him control me any longer. He hated being disobeyed. Jimmy reached down and grabbed Jeffrey and headed for the front door. Mom tried to pull Jeffrey out of his grasp to keep Jimmy from taking the child. It became a bizarre game of Tug of War with Jeffrey being pulled back and forth. Before the toddler could be physically hurt, my mom let go. Jimmy loaded the child into his car and left.

Mom and I were very worried about Jeffrey's safety, so we drove over to the house with the plan of getting him back. Jimmy had always made it clear he was never going to "babysit" his son. It had been a couple of hours since they left Mom's, I believed he would be more than willing to give Jeffrey back to me. I used my key to open the front door, but Jimmy had nailed the door shut and would not let us in. We tried to reason with Jimmy through the door and windows but he ignored us. We could hear Jeffrey laughing and playing inside and believed he was safe for the time being.

Mom and I drove back to her house and called the Sacramento County Sheriff's Department. I explained the history of Jimmy's behavior and the violence. The sheriff asked if we were legally separated or divorced, and I had to admit that we were not separated or divorced. The sheriff then said, "He's the dad. There is no court order and he has just as much right to the child as you do." Father's rights and joint custody of children were just becoming a hot topic back then. The sheriff assured me "there was nothing he could do" and suggested "I stay at my mom's until things calmed down."

I knew right then I needed to get a divorce and needed to get some legal custody papers. I needed legal rights to my child. All this took place on a Saturday, so I could not do anything about it until the courts opened again until Monday morning.

Jimmy never told me he was leaving town with our son. He never told anyone except my dad and Jacky his wife. What he did tell me was to never come home again because I was no longer welcome in our home.

Sunday morning Jimmy packed two suitcases, grabbed the wedding album, and drove to the Sacramento airport. Without telling anyone, he and Jeffrey boarded a Delta Airlines airplane and headed to his hometown, Bristol, Tennessee. He told his family we were all moving to Bristol. When I never showed up, he told them there was a change, and I would be arriving later in the month after my college semester

57

was over. When they grew skeptical, Jimmy kept assuring them I was coming. He told them I would be there before Christmas. They were excited their brother and his family were finally moving home to Tennessee.

December 1978 was the worst month of my life. Monday morning I met with an attorney I found in the yellow pages. My mom paid the $300 retainer fee because I had no money of my own. Mom and I met with the attorney. He made it very clear each parent had equal rights because there were no formal custody orders. He strongly encouraged me to go get Jeffrey and bring him back to California. During these troubled times, I continued to attend college and was close to earning my Associate of Arts (AA) degree. Because school was out for the holidays, I was free to put all my efforts into getting my child home safely.

Mom was still working for both A.G. Spanos and Alex, two highly influential Greek businessmen, who were like family. They knew my mom and I were stressed and very worried about Jeffrey's safety. It was agreed that a mutual friend, Gus, would fly with me back to Tennessee and together we would get Jeffrey and bring him back to California. Because there were no formal legal agreements, it would not be kidnapping. It was important that I be the one taking Jeffrey because I was the mom.

We looked for flights where we could fly in, have a few hours in the middle of the day, and fly out by late evening. The plan was to leave early in the morning, get Jeffrey and fly home on the "red eye" the same night.

Every day I talked with Jimmy's sister Debbie. She knew me from the times we visited and was excited we were moving out to Tennessee. Debbie was a very kind, gracious, and simple Christian woman. She seemed to love everyone, especially her family. I really liked her and felt terrible about lying to her and tricking her into telling me about Jimmy's daily routines with Jeffrey.

Debbie told me Jimmy left every day to be with his friends and cousins. She had concerns about Jimmy's excessive drinking. She babysat Jeffrey all day everyday. She told me to hurry up and get out there so Jimmy would settle down and be a good husband and father. She was doing everything for Jeffrey, feeding him, reading him stories, doing his laundry, putting him down for naps, entertaining him, and taking him to Sunday school.

When Jeffrey needed clothes, Debbie bought them. She also purchased some toys for him to play with. She was trying to be the perfect fill-in mother until I got there. I assured her I was coming, but I did not know exactly when. I made it clear there were loose ends to finish up in California. I needed time to get our plans into action.

Without telling any of his family, Jimmy made an appointment with an attorney. He told the attorney we had agreed to move to Tennessee. Then he told the attorney I changed my mind and refused to move back there with him. The attorney told Jimmy I had violated a Tennessee law, and they filed abandonment charges against me. They hired a process server in California. I was served a subpoena just hours before Gus and I were leaving for the airport.

My mom's doorbell rang, and when I opened the door, a man asked my name then handed me a manila envelope. "What this?" I asked. He turned and said "You've been served." I opened the envelope and could not believe what I was reading. My nightmare never seemed to have an ending. I was being charged with abandoning my child, in Tennessee a felony punishable with possible jail time. How could this be happening?

I collapsed into a chair and sobbed. Mom told Gus the flight to Tennessee was off. I called my lawyer and explained my subpoena and asked for guidance. My attorney explained there were 13 states in the United States that did not extradite parents back to the home state during divorce procedures. Tennessee was one of those 13 states. Jimmy got to court first, so his court order took priority. I had a date and time to appear in a Tennessee court. A Tennessee judge would determine Jeffrey's and my fates.

I did not have a good feeling at all about any of this. I had a fear that if I went back to Tennessee with no family support, I might never return to California. I needed time to think and needed time to come up with a new plan. I knew Jimmy was never going to be able to function as a single parent. His sister Debbie had taken over full responsibility for Jeffrey, including tucking him in at night.

I decided to call his bluff. I told him I was not coming to Tennessee for court, and I was not moving to Tennessee. Half way through the conversation Jimmy said he only got the court order so my mother could not influence me to stay in California. I kept telling him "You win. Take good care of our son. Don't let him forget me."

I made it very clear that I was not ever moving to Tennessee, and he would be responsible for raising Jeffrey. I could feel him starting to panic. His sister Debbie had already told him he needed to be more responsible for his son. They had been staying with Debbie and her family for nearly three weeks. Jimmy, according to Debbie, was coming home to her house drunk every night. She had a strong no drinking policy around herself and her family. Jimmy was ignoring every rule and disregarding every value she had.

Debbie was a strong woman of faith. She told me she was trying to be patient with Jimmy until I got there. What she didn't know was I was never going back there. I hoped that with Jimmy's support system crumbling down around him, he would get scared and bring Jeffrey back.

I continued to work with my attorney in California. I looked for a good attorney in Tennessee. By now Gus was out of the picture. Since I was subpoenaed, there was a temporary court order so we could not grab Jeffrey and bring him back to California legally. They would have been able to file kidnapping charges against us. I was on my own again working alone against the system.

Jimmy and Jeffrey celebrated Christmas with Debbie and her family. She made sure Jeffrey had lots of presents from the family and from Santa Claus. I spoke with my small son on Christmas morning and it was one of the hardest conversations I have ever had. He was so happy telling me everything Santa had brought him. It tore my heart out to not be with him. I was glad he was doing well and will forever be grateful to Debbie for taking wonderful care of him.

Next Jimmy got on the phone and begged me to come back to him in Tennessee. He tried to entice me with the promise of finding us a nice home. With all the strength I had inside me I told him, "No." I was not moving to Tennessee.

Just before Christmas, his sister Barbara had decided to leave Sacramento and move back to Tennessee. Years before she relocated to Sacramento, she had lost custody of her two minor sons to her in-laws. She decided to return to Tennessee to fight for custody of her young sons.

Her family went to court with her to offer support. Jimmy, Debbie, and some other relatives sat in the courtroom. After a short hearing, Barbara was denied custody and visitations with her minor sons. She fell apart in the courtroom and was crying as her sons were asked to leave the courtroom with their grandparents.

Barbara went out into the courthouse hallway and totally broke down. She cried, howled, screamed, and fell to the floor. It was reported to me that the cries were gut wrenching. Jimmy could not handle the pain his sister was feeling. Then he started crying, howling, and sobbing. He started saying, "Oh my God, what have I done to Julie?" Debbie asked Jimmy to explain to her what was going on because she was confused. He then spilled his guts and told her the whole story. The entire truth. Jimmy took ownership of everything he had done.

Debbie was furious and said she felt duped. As a strong Christian woman, she wanted to be helpful but resented being lied to. She told Jimmy right there in the courthouse hallway that he needed to step up and be a father. She made it clear she was stepping down as the primary caretaker of Jeffrey.

She left the courthouse, went home and called me telling me the entire story and asked for my forgiveness. We cried and I asked for her forgiveness for making her believe I was coming back. Debbie said she thought I should stay in California, and she would do everything in her power to convince Jimmy to bring Jeffrey home to me. I did not tell her I had two lawyers, one in California and one in Tennessee. We were developing a plan. The plan was to get Jeffrey back home to California safely and legally.

Without telling anyone in his family, Jimmy packed up Jeffrey, and they flew home to California on

December 28, 1978. When they landed at the Sacramento Airport it was mid-afternoon. Jimmy stopped off at the bar and had a few drinks. He let Jeffrey run around. A security guard told him minors were not allowed in the airport bar. Jimmy started mouthing off to the security guard as he was being escorted out of the airport.

Since the incident over Thanksgiving weekend at the bar, our co-worker John had received a promotion. He was now a supervisor over the custodians at the airport. John was a Filipino man who always wore a hat and dark glasses. His new job required him to wear a business suit. As Jimmy was being escorted out, John was walking towards him. Jimmy became very agitated yelling, "Let's finish what we started downtown." He then hit John, knocking his hat and glasses to the floor. Jeffrey was wandering about, and some strangers gathered him up and kept him safe and out of harm's way.

The security guard collected Jeffrey and continued to escort Jimmy out of the airport. When they stopped to get the luggage, it was missing. The airline lost the luggage and it was never found. All the clothes were lost forever.

The only reason I heard this story in detail is because airport security called to make sure Jeffrey was returned to me safely. The security guard told me the story and asked me to make a complete inventory of Jeffrey's belongings. The airline eventually paid for a total replacement of his clothing.

No charges were filed against Jimmy. The security guard said he was thankful everyone arrived home safely because Jimmy was very drunk.

# Chapter 7

# Hiding Out

Because we didn't know that Jimmy was bringing Jeffrey back to California, I was still working on my plans to get Jeffrey back. The Tennessee attorney, and my California attorney both had a clear understanding of the entire situation. We all agreed I needed to fly to Tennessee and tell the judge my side of the story. The Tennessee courts were closed for the Christmas holidays and were only taking emergency cases. A court date was set for early January. My mom insisted she would be traveling with me. We immediately began making travel arrangements with a local travel agent.

On the evening of December 28th there was a knock at the front door. Mom looked out the window and couldn't see a car in the driveway. She went to the door and asked who it was. She heard a muffled voice that sounded like "Jimmy." Mom swung the door open there stood Jimmy and Jeffrey. My mom screamed "Oh my God! Julie, come quickly!" I came running down the hall, and there was my son in my mother's arms. I reached for him, and Jeffrey leaped towards me and grabbed tightly onto my neck. He would not let go. I started crying but Jeffrey was laughing. He was so excited to see me. Then he wanted down, and as soon as his feet hit the ground he ran around giving Dennis and Anna big hugs.

After hugging everyone, Jeffrey went to his toy box and played. No one spoke to Jimmy. All of our attention was on Jeffrey. We all sat silently, privately trying to come up with a new plan. It was clearer than ever how unpredictable Jimmy's behavior had become. No one wanted to spook him. Going to court in California was a dream come true. Finally, something was going my way. In my heart, I really believed Jimmy had returned to California to give Jeffrey back to me.

We all waited patiently for Jimmy to leave, but he never did. After nearly three hours I said "It's late, and we need to get to bed." Jimmy said "You're right, it is getting late." Relief swept through my body, heart, and soul. This nightmare of mine was almost over. Then Jimmy scooped Jeffrey up, packed up his things, and said, "Good-bye." "What?" I screamed, "Leave him here with me." I pleaded and begged, arguing I had not seen my son for over a month. Jimmy replied, "Come home with me, and I will give him to you." I knew going back to that house was not an option for me. I let go of my son and watched them leave.

The next morning, I called the Tennessee attorney and apprised him of the situation. Next, I called my California attorney and did the same thing. My local attorney immediately got a court date scheduled in Divorce Court. Again, because of the holidays and the back-log in the courts, my date was scheduled for late January. While I was on the phone with the attorney, Jimmy knocked on my mom's front door.

I hung up the phone, opened the front door, and Jimmy said, "Jeffrey needs breakfast and a bath." I fed my son, then gave him a long bath, giving him time to play and me time to think. I dressed Jeffrey and did my best to normalize the terrible situation for my son. I did not want Jeffrey traumatized any more than he already was. Then without any warning Jimmy said, "I have to go." As he left the house, I again thought he had finally come to his senses and was giving Jeffrey back to me for good.

My mom was at work talking with Mr. Spanos on the phone. They were working hard to come up with a getaway plan for me and Jeffrey. It was decided I would hide out in a vacant apartment outside of Fair Oaks. Jimmy also had worked for the Spanos Corporation, so I needed to be placed in a complex unfamiliar to Jimmy.

Jimmy kept coming and going from Mom's house about every 30 minutes. He did this all morning and into the afternoon. He needed sleep and was physically exhausted. My emotions were all over the map. He was still controlling me. I was being emotionally terrorized. I felt hopeful and helpless. I felt strong and weak. I felt powerful and scared to death. I had one good shot left to get my son to safety, and I was not going to blow it.

Friday night December 29th, Jimmy left again with our son, taking him back to our house. Part of me believed I should surrender and go home to be with Jeffrey. The other part knew if I went back, the next time Jimmy got mad he would probably kill me.

Saturday morning at 7:00 a.m., Jimmy again brought Jeffrey over for breakfast and a bath. I fed Jeffrey but did not get him dressed right away. He did not have much clothing because of the lost luggage at the airport. I kept Jeffrey in his footed one piece pajamas so he would be warm and could play. Jimmy left saying he had things to do.

My mom left for work that morning as usual. She kept calling to see how we were doing. I had no idea she was at work developing an escape plan for me. It was decided there was no suitable and safe Spanos apartment for us to stay in. Mom and my godmother Thelma found a family member's empty condo in South Sacramento that was ready to sell. The owner agreed to hold off listing it until my court date in January was over.

Auntie Nora had her 1964 Ford Mustang hidden and parked at Mr. Givens' house, a neighbor up the hill. Her son Dan was prepared to be my driver. One set of neighbors, Tim and Doris, bought and packed a suitcase full of toddler clothes. Another purchased Huggies diapers and had hid them along with the clothes in the Mustang. Dennis sat in his truck prepared to block Jimmy if he showed up when Dan came to pick me up and drive me to the condo.

I had no idea all this was going on. I was quietly trying to come up with my own plan. Jimmy's comings and goings were getting more spread out. That morning he left at 8:00 a.m. and did not return until noon. My mom called to see what was going on. I explained the situation. She told me to call her immediately when he left and to have Jeffrey packed. She said we were going shopping to get him some new clothes. I was suspicious and began questioning her. Mom sternly said, "Do as I say," and she hung up on me.

Mom's office was seven minutes from her home, maybe less on a Saturday with little traffic. Jimmy left about 12:30 p.m., and almost immediately Uncle Ed came over. He said, "Your mom called and wants to make sure you are getting ready to go shopping." Then Auntie Nora came over and explained that I was leaving for a safe location right now.

Jimmy was always extra intuitive when it came to me. He was hiding at the bottom of the hill to the west. He walked back towards the house. He saw everyone gathered in the street as we were getting ready to start the move. Jimmy started running and yelling, "That's my son! That's my son!" Auntie Nora ran home, called Mr. Givens' to relay a message to her son Dan to get the car started and wait at the top of the very long driveway. Dan was expecting to drive down the hill, pick me up, and have a quiet uneventful transportation duty taking me to my new living quarters.

My mom, also being extra intuitive, rushed home via the hill on the east side. She flew down the street in her car screaming out her window to Dennis, "We need you!" Mom and Dennis came screeching around the corner to the family house. Uncle Ed, Auntie Nora, and Tim had Jimmy surrounded. Mom screamed at me to run up the field to Mr. Givens' house. I had no clue what was happening or what I was supposed to do. Grabbing Jeffrey, I took off running through Auntie Nora's yard to a hill on Mr. Givens' property. The hill was steep, and Mr. Givens had just finished running a rototiller over the ground. Sinking up to my ankles in soft dirt, I felt like I was in quicksand. I kept falling down. Looking back over the rooftops, I could see Jimmy being held back by my friends and family, and he could see me. I knew if I did not keep moving I might never escape this man.

I was having flashbacks to the night at the bar. But this time I was being protected by people who loved me, people who were helping me, and people who were my family. Not escaping was not an option. I struggled in the soft dirt but kept moving forward.

When I reached the top of what felt like a huge mountain, I was both physically and emotionally drained. I saw Dan sitting in the car with the engine running. He had no idea what was going on. He saw the desperate look on my face, jumped out of the car, grabbed Jeffrey, and helped us get into the car. I yelled, "We have to go now! Dan, get in the car. He's coming." He jumped in, and we sped backwards down the long driveway, tires screeching.

Jimmy had run back to his car and raced up to Mr. Givens' driveway. Just as we hit the main road, I saw

71

Jimmy's car speeding towards us. Then I saw Dennis and his little yellow Plymouth Arrow Sport pick-up truck speed up and pull in front of Jimmy's car, blocking him, and giving Dan, Jeffrey, and me time to get away. Jimmy jumped out of his car and ran towards Mom's house, taking short cuts through people's yards. Dan drove down to our street, and as we passed by the houses the parents were yelling, "GO!" We raced off, and we could see Uncle Ed and Tim in the rear-view window restraining Jimmy.

Dan drove us quickly down to South Sacramento and dropped Jeffrey and me off at the empty two bedroom condo. Within an hour of us being dropped off, my Godparents arrived with two folding lawn chairs and a television set. They stayed for about an hour, getting us settled in.

Mom was able to get the utilities all turned on by phone. Later that evening, Mom and Dennis brought down cots, blankets, pillows, food, kitchen supplies, clothes for me and Jeffrey, toys, lamps, and a potted yellow chrysanthemum. She said I needed a bright spot to focus on. Mom always tried to make a bad situation brighter for me. At that time I did not appreciate the gesture as an act of love and support. Looking back, I understand it was just one of the many ways my mom saved and supported me.

We were staying in this condo until the court date. I needed to obtain a temporary custody order and a restraining order. In the beginning, things were great. I was relaxing and unwinding because I felt safe. Jimmy did not know where we were. Jeffrey and I were getting back into our old routines. We were laughing, talking, and playing little games. Finally, we were getting free of this horrible mess. Things were looking up.

The next afternoon, Mom and Dennis brought me a loaner car borrowed from friends. They also brought casseroles and other food from family and friends. The goal was to relax, unwind, and get ready for court. Saturday night went well. Sunday night around 11:00 p.m., Jeffrey had a horrible screaming night terror. He seemed asleep but was screaming and sobbing at the top of his lungs. Monday night again around 11:00 p.m., he had another screaming night terror. This one lasted longer than the night before. I was unable to wake him up or calm him down. We were both crying. We both had been terrorized, and the nightmare was nowhere over for us.

The neighbors in the condo became concerned and called the police, reporting a screaming child. Two Sacramento police officers showed up at the door. I explained what had been going on all the way back to the previous Thanksgiving weekend. They radioed in to their dispatcher and verified Jimmy had been placed under arrest a couple of times. The police officers were wonderful with Jeffrey. They talked kindly to him and stayed until he was back to sleep on his cot.

Tuesday there was another night terror. Each night terror seemed louder and lasted longer than the one before. I was afraid the neighbors would call the police again. Eventually Jeffrey calmed down, but this particular night he would not go back to sleep. He was restless and this was making me restless. I did some deep thinking, then said to myself, "This is bullshit." I packed up our clothes, toys, personal items, and our potted plant, and we headed back to Fair Oaks.

I had no idea where we were going and had about an hour to come up with a plan. Jeffrey was having night terrors each night around 11:00 p.m. and it was nearly midnight by the time I decided to leave. My Godmother's daughter Luann had given me a key to her house and encouraged me to use it anytime I wanted to. This home was on the same property as my Godparent's home. Luann's teenage daughter was my babysitter when I worked nights at the county. Jeffrey was used to falling asleep in their home and felt safe and comfortable there. I needed help and support, and I knew they would welcome us. I used my key, then I made a bed on the couch for me and Jeffrey. That was the last night Jeffrey had night terrors.

In the morning, I realized I needed a more workable plan. I called Mom and explained about the night terrors and the police interaction. My friend Clarissa lived with her parents and invited us to stay with them. Clarissa was a friend I had met while attending American River College. She was a child development major and worked at the childcare center where Jeffrey attended on campus. We had become fast friends. She hated Jimmy, and he hated her. Because of this mutual hatred, Jimmy did not know where she lived. I decided to stay with them until I went to court. I called my attorney, and he was able to get an emergency court date within the week.

I only had three days to wait before I would go before a judge. Again, I started to relax. I walked into their kitchen out of view of Jeffrey and he let out a blood curdling scream. He was panicking, couldn't catch his breath, and would not stop crying or screaming. My son's night terrors were now full blown day terrors. I realized Jeffrey had a fear I was leaving him, and he would never see me again. I am convinced now this was Post Traumatic Stress Disorder (PTSD). Every time Jeffrey could not find me, he was being re-traumatized. Watching him suffer was breaking my heart.

We needed to prove to Jeffrey I was not leaving him ever. I got in my car, drove around a short block, leaving Jeffrey on the front lawn with Clarissa. I drove away watching him in my rear view mirror crying out, "Momma, Momma." At first I returned almost immediately. We did this until it started becoming a game for him. Then we made the absence last longer, about two or three minutes. Each time I returned I would get out of the car, open my arms, and give Jeffrey a long loving hug. After a few minutes I'd leave again. This routine went on for hours.

Eventually Jeffrey got into the spirit and started waiting for my return. Each time he got comfortable, I would stretch out my time away. Later, we moved him into the house, and I left again. His panic attacks immediately returned. I returned through the front door, wrapping him in a huge loving hug with a warm greeting. We repeated this until Jeffrey got the message loud and clear that no matter what, I was always coming back. We had successfully desensitized him from the fear of being separated from me, his mom. There were no more night terrors or day terrors after that weekend.

We stayed with Clarissa and her family for the next three days until I was able to go court. The judge granted me full "physical custody," and he granted us both "joint medical and legal custody." Jimmy was granted visitation on his days off from Sunday at noon until Monday evening at 5:00 p.m. Jimmy was told he could not drink four hours before or during a visit. He could not take Jeffrey out of state without permission from the court, and he was warned he better not violate the current order of protection. Jimmy never exercised his visitation rights.

Jimmy was ordered to pay $125 per month in child support and one dollar per month for 18 months in alimony. Jimmy yelled quite loudly in court, "I will go to hell before I pay her one dollar in alimony." I must say he was true to his word on that statement. However, he didn't pay child support either.

After court, I moved in with my mom, sister, and Dennis until I could find permanent housing for myself and my child. I applied for and received welfare services. My monthly cash grant was $330. In addition, I received food stamps and Medi-Cal benefits. I was still attending college and planned to graduate at the end of the semester; therefore, I also had money from my Federal Pell grant.

I started looking for places to live. Most apartments required first and last month's rent and a cleaning deposit. I had very little monthly income and no savings. Most low-cost Housing Urban Development (HUD) housing units had a year waiting list. I was desperate and needed help immediately.

I took a chance and stopped by the Kenneth Arms Apartment Complex in Carmichael because they had low income and HUD certified units. I explained my situation to the office manager, hoping to get on the list for a low income unit. She put my name at the top of her HUD waiting list. She said one bedroom low income and HUD units usually became available fairly often. Because my son was under age six, we could share a one bedroom unit even though we were of the opposite sex. He was under three at the time. The manager said after we moved in, she would move me to a two bedroom unit when one became vacant.

At the end of January, the apartment manager called to ask if I wanted to move into an upstairs one bedroom unit on the first of February. She explained I would be under the HUD program which meant my rent and utilities would be 10 percent of my income, only $33. I screamed into the phone, "Yes I would!"

I had two weeks to gather up a few pieces of furniture and some household goods. I already had new clothing for Jeffrey from our friends and the money the airline gave me for the lost luggage. My friends and family gave us some extra furniture and household goods. They also helped us move in on the first of the month. Our new apartment was beautiful, safe, and full of love. I knew we could be comfortable here for years, and I was excited to be free at last.

A month or so later, we had another date in family court. I was afraid to have a face to face with Jimmy. I knew I had my attorney, and I knew the judge and bailiff would be present, but I was scared to death. Jimmy had not had any visits with our son since the last hearing. Through his attorney, he requested joint physical custody of Jeffrey. My attorney reminded the judge of the recent violence, but the judge made it very clear, "Jimmy is the child's father and in California both parents should have equal access to their children."

Joint custody was fairly new, and the courts were bending over backwards to be fair to fathers. The judge ordered a child custody recommendation hearing. That meant a social worker would be interviewing us both and would make a recommendation to the judge regarding "the best interest of the child." I was told a social worker would be calling me for an appointment, and I would need to bring my son into their office.

Jeffrey and I were settling nicely into our new apartment, and it was beautiful. We had neighbors who became our friends and are still our friends to this day. Life was good. I was almost done with my Associate of Arts (AA) degree. Jeffrey was going to college with me and being cared for at the ARC Childcare Center.

In our one bedroom apartment, I had a queen size bed. Jeffrey and I could have easily shared the same bed, but I wanted him to have a space of his own. The apartment had two large closets, one in the bedroom and one in the kitchen. I turned the bedroom closet into a room for Jeffrey using a puffy chaise lounge pad that filled the entire closet floor and made it up into a bed with sheets and his favorite blanket. Remember, Jeffrey was not yet three years old. We taped his drawings from daycare onto the wall. It was great! During the day, the door was closed, and at night the door was open. My bed and his bed were close together. He had his own space, and he could easily see me.

Three days after being in court, the doorbell rang at 7:00 a.m. I did not have telephone service because my budget was tight. I thought Jimmy had found out where we lived and was coming to harass and hurt me. My heart was pounding, and I couldn't catch my breath. I knew the neighbors were still home, so I aggressively swung the door open and said, "Yes?" There stood a male stranger. I asked, "May I help you?" The man said, "I'm Ron Saylor from Sacramento County Family Court. I'm here to do a home study for the joint custody recommendation hearing." I must say, I felt a bit set up since I was told I would be meeting a social worker in the courthouse office with my child.

Mr. Saylor immediately started talking with Jeffrey, asking questions, while he wrote things down on his clipboard. Both Jeffrey and I were in our pajamas. Luckily, I keep a clean house, and everything looked nice and neat. After about 20 minutes, Mr. Saylor was getting ready to leave until Jeffrey asked him if he wanted to see his room. Mr. Saylor knew our apartment was a one bedroom and immediately asked, "Where do you sleep?" "In the closet," Jeffrey answered. Mr. Saylor sat up straighter and began taking lots of notes. My heart was pounding rapidly. I felt good about my decision when I made it, but under the brutal eye of the court, I was questioning that decision.

Eventually, Mr. Saylor and Jeffrey walked backed to the bedroom and Jeffrey slid open the closet door. Inside the closet was a cute little room. His bed was made up, stuffed animals were lined up along the wall, his pictures were hung up at eye level, glow-in-the-dark stars were affixed to the walls, and his little outfits were folded on the top shelves.

All of a sudden I did not care what the court officer said or thought about my closet. It was a brilliant idea, and I was sticking with my decision to give my son his own space. In the end Mr. Saylor said he was not going to mention the "closet room" in his notes and added he thought my idea was awesome. He also said "his own child would love to have a special little room." After he left, I felt very good about my chances to get full custody of my son. When we went back before the judge, I was granted full physical custody, and Jimmy and I were awarded joint medical and legal custody.

# Chapter 8

# A Victim With No Voice

Finally it was time for me to graduate from American River College. I was so excited and could not wait to rent my graduation robe and "walk" in the graduation ceremony. I had earned my diploma, and I and I was anxious to get it. It had been a very long five years since I graduated from high school. So much had happened since then.

My parents were divorced. My sister Anna, was 18 years old and was graduating from high school. I was a single mom of a three year old son, and we were finally doing well. I was thrilled about finishing college and sharing my pride and accomplishment with my family.

I ordered my graduation robe and was getting ready to order my graduation announcements. Before I finalized the order, my mom called. "Julie, I just got a notice from Anna's school. Mark your calendar. Her graduation is in June." The date my mom gave me was the exact date of my college graduation, only three hours earlier. I very quietly told my mom "that is my graduation day". She asked me what time the graduation was, and I told her 6:00 p.m. Mom said, "Well, we can't do both, and you need to be at the high school because this is a very big deal for Anna." WOW!

I did not know what to say. I wanted to scream, "Hey! This is a very big deal for me too." But I did not have the confidence to say those words out loud.

We all gathered in the front of the high school on the afternoon of Anna's graduation. She surprised us all when she appeared wearing a red robe. This meant she had an honors level grade point average. She had worked hard in school, had done well, and was being rewarded with a red robe. We were all very proud of her.

Both our parents and their partners attended to show their support for Anna. After the ceremony, Anna was so excited when she found out her friends were all going out together to celebrate. She begged my mom to let her go with them. Mom explained that we were all going out to dinner. In typical kid style, Anna relentlessly begged to go with her friends. Mom finally said "yes, fine, go."

My dad and his wife had already left. I stood on the sidewalk talking with my mom and her fiancé Dennis. We were expressing our pride over Anna's accomplishments. Then mom and Dennis said good-bye and left. As I stood on the sidewalk alone, I looked down at my watch and wondered if it was too late to attend my own graduation ceremony. American River College was just eight miles down the road, and the ceremony was set to start in about 45 minutes. At that moment I felt invisible, unimportant, and very alone. To compensate for my loneliness, I drove myself right over to "Ah Chop Chop," a greasy

Chinese food drive-through restaurant. I went home and ate Chicken Chow Mein, and it helped ease my pain for a little while. As the sun went down on my apartment and I was eating alone in the dark, I realized I was still a victim with no voice. After all I had gone through, how could that be?

Later I learned that I suffered from Intimate Partner Violence (IPV), an abuse that refers specifically to violence between partners who have an intimate relationship. A victim of IVP, according to the U.S. Department of Veterans Affairs National Center for PTSD, can fall under any of these five categories:

- Physical violence: Hitting, pushing, grabbing, biting, choking/strangulating, shaking, slapping, kicking, hair pulling, or restraining.
- Sexual violence: Attempted or actual sexual contact when the partner does not want to or is unable to consent (for example, when affected by alcohol or illness).
- Threats of physical or sexual abuse: Ways to cause fear through words, looks, actions or weapons.
- Psychological or emotional abuse: Name calling, humiliating, putting you down, keeping you from friends and family, bullying, controlling where you go, or what you wear.
- Stalking: Following, harassing, or unwanted contact that makes you feel afraid.

Some people experience only one of these forms of violence while others experience many types of violence. IPV can be a single event or last for many years. I was a victim of all five categories, and it took a great deal of time and effort on my part to learn how to quit being a victim. No one deserves to be treated this way, and that included me. I needed and wanted to find my own voice.

There is no magic pill. Behavior change takes hard work, dedication, and the strong desire to make changes. I signed up for every free Domestic Violence seminar, self-help therapy, and group therapy session I could find. I checked self-help books out of the library. I enrolled in a Divorce Recovery workshop at a church. I attended Overeaters Anonymous meetings, and I went to Alcoholics Anonymous meetings trying to understand alcoholics and their behaviors. I found teachers, coaches, friends, and mentors who would help guide me to a healthier life path.

I took my son to therapy through the school district because he was having some mild behavioral issues at school. I was shocked when Jo, the therapist, saw me instead of him. Jo said, "I work with the parents until the children get well." I saw her every Wednesday afternoon from September through June. I felt blessed that my therapist had terrific insight and helped me to grow into a better and stronger woman.

Domestic violence is like a tornado that leaves behind a trail of destruction. It can flatten the lives of women and children. It takes away self-confidence, self-esteem, and self-worth. It creates an environment of fear, confusion, bitterness, and mistrust. Feelings of shame often grow. I asked myself the hard questions. "How did I get into this mess, and why couldn't I get myself out?" It was clear I needed to make some personal life changes to better myself and my life. Changing my thinking, feeling, and gut reactions was hard work. Change didn't come automatically just because I wished it would, wanted it to, or thought it should. Coming up with a plan and committing to the plan was the only way my life was going to get better.

My first step in taking personal responsibility was to learn what I could about domestic violence. I needed to know what it actually was and how it was impacting my life. I knew I felt shame, guilt, and I was very weak in mind and spirit. I was totally exhausted. I knew I needed to understand the cause in order to make the changes in myself that I wanted to make.

# Chapter 9

# Domestic Violence

Battering, wife-beating, partner abuse, woman abuse, person abuse, husband abuse, and child abuse are all violent actions committed against another person within the home and are considered domestic violence.

Domestic violence is about power and control where one person needs to control the thoughts and behaviors of another person or persons. When the abuser feels he cannot get control, the abuse increases and intensifies over time. The abuser believes he knows best and wants to make all the decisions because he wants all the power. The abused partner feels and believes she is left with limited freedom to make personal decisions for herself. The abused partner feels and believes there is no way out of the situation.

Abusive relationships can sound very similar, but each abusive relationship is unique to each individual. My story could be very different from another person's story. We all have our own personal history. Abusive behaviors include the use of threats, coercion, rape, force, economic exploitation, devaluing, beatings, bruising, biting, grabbing, sexual humiliation, being hit or slapped, and emotional or psychological abuse.

Acts of domestic violence generally fall into one or more of these categories:

- Psychological Battering: Psychological or mental violence can include constant verbal abuse, name calling, threats, harassment, excessive possessiveness, isolating the woman from friends and family, deprivation of physical and economic resources, destruction of personal property and pets, use of children as a means of control, stalking, or using violence in the abused woman's presence, for example, punching a fist through a wall.

- Physical Battering: Physical attacks or aggressive behavior can range from bruising to murder, often beginning with acts that are excused as trivial, such as restraining, pushing, slapping or pinching. Later the abuser often escalates into more frequent and serious attacks such as punching, kicking, biting, sexual assault, tripping, throwing, or hitting. Eventually the abuse may lead to life-threatening behaviors such as choking, breaking bones or using weapons, often resulting in fatal injury to the woman and her children.

- Sexual Abuse: Attacks are often accompanied by, or culminate in, sexual violence wherein the woman is forced to have sexual intercourse with her abuser, take part in unwanted sexual activity, or experience sexual humiliation.

A large percent of abuse is committed by men towards women. There is not a typical woman who will be abused. Regardless of race, gender, age, class, or economic status, it can happen to anyone. Accessibility to local resources is crucial to helping someone who is being abused.

Black, blue, and swollen eyes are never an acceptable look when an abuser is the culprit. Someone I love dearly was attacked by her husband. They had not lived together for over three years. She had been trying to get a divorce the entire time. They have two small children, and he does not want a separation or a divorce. He stalls matters in court even to the point of firing his attorney and acting on his own behalf. She has had several protective orders against him, yet he is able to talk his way out of trouble.

This abuser is a single dad of three children from a previous marriage, has a college degree, and a great paying job. He belongs to a church with strict codes of conduct on how a family is to operate. He is buying his home and looks presentable to the public. For years he has been able to convince police officers, his attorney, and the court that she is the liar, and he is the victim. In reality he is a bully, and he has abused his wife very badly.

The last abuse took place after he hung out on the sidewalk in front of her house waiting for her older kids to walk out the front door to go play. He walked up her walkway and entered her home. She freaked out when she saw him and ordered him to get out of her house. He refused to leave and began yelling out orders stating, "You are still my wife, and you will listen to me!" She started calling 911 on her cell phone. In an attempt to get the phone away from her, he grabbed her around the neck and began choking her and punching her in the face.

Eventually he left, and she was able to complete her call to the police. The officer believed her story and went to her husband's house and arrested him. She then went to the Emergency Room to get checked out. They did a CT scan, and luckily nothing was broken this time.

The abuser's bail was posted at $1,500 cash only. He was released from jail before she was released from the Emergency Room. All this happened on a Saturday night, and the first thing Monday morning she got another Order of Protection from the court.

Anyone can be a victim of domestic violence. It is an extremely traumatizing experience. For many, the psychological scars and pain far outlast the physical pain. Many people who have been abused suffer from Post-Traumatic Stress Disorder (PTSD), heightened anxiety, and severe stress. It is not uncommon to have flashbacks, nightmares, anxiety attacks, panic attacks, feelings of emotional numbness, a great sense of danger much of the time, or to have problems sleeping, causing sleep deprivation.

Breaking the fear and isolation of domestic violence takes planning and follow through on the survivor's part. Seeking out a good counselor or support group is a must. The survivor does not have to go through recovery alone. Talking to friends, family, and other domestic abuse survivors will help victims move forward.

Finding a good counselor is a must. Counselors provide a safe, non-judgmental place to express fears, doubts, feelings, goals, hopes and thoughts. A counselor might make a referral to a medical doctor to help control some of the symptoms of anxiety. Investing sufficient time with a good counselor can make it possible to move on and create a life that allows a woman to be the best version of herself. She should not be afraid to change counselors if her needs are not being met.

Here are some issues that may develop after abuse:

- Anxiety: Survivors may be afraid of others who remind them of their abuser. They might be fearful of being alone. Experiencing panic attacks is not uncommon.
- Anger: Survivors may be angry at themselves for getting abused or angry at others who could have helped them.
- Post-traumatic stress disorder (PTSD): Survivors may have reoccurring nightmares, flashbacks, fears, or panic attacks.
- Shame: Survivors may think they caused the abuse or deserved it.

- <u>Trust</u>: Trusting others may become difficult. Survivors may have difficulty learning how to trust again.

- <u>Self-abuse</u>: Survivors of abuse may engage in self-destructive behaviors such as self-medicating with drugs or alcohol, cutting or burning themselves, neglecting personal hygiene, or having sex with anyone and everyone.

- <u>Dissociation</u>: Survivors may lack any feelings at all, may feel numb, confused, or may get repressed to where the survivor has no memory at all of the abuse.

Stress can be dangerous to your health. People think and talk about stress all the time. For example, you might be stressed about a test, your bills, your marriage, your health, or your inability to sleep because stress is keeping you awake at night. Many people use the word stress when their feelings become too overwhelming to deal with.

Most people are reacting to a "stressor," the agent causing the stress when they say they are stressed. Stress is what your body feels and reacts to. For example, when you feel anxious, your blood pressure goes up, breathing becomes more rapid, and your heart-rate rises. This is stress. The stressor is something that caused the stress, such as the exam you are hoping to pass, your partner having an affair, or the large amount of debt you have is the stressor. When there are a lot of stressors present, a person's level of stress becomes quite large and begins to feel unmanageable.

We need some stress in our lives otherwise we could die or get hurt. The body picks up on danger signals and activates to protect. It either tells you to run or to stay and fight. This is called the "fight-or-flight response" an instinctive physiological response to a threatening situation, which readies one either to resist forcibly or to run away. It was first described by Walter Bradford Cannon in the 1920s when he was studying animals whose survival was being threatened. It is also known as "acute stress response" because it prepares the body for one of two reactions to a threat, to fight or to run.

All stress is not bad. Years ago when I met my current husband and we started dating, I became very stressed out. I remember one night waiting for him to pick me up for a date. My dress was pretty, I was having a good hair day, and we were going to a fun Valentine's Day event in the community. I really liked this guy and so did my family. I thought he might "be the one."

Without any warning, I started to cry hysterically and not the pretty little cry with a few tears spilling out my eyes. This was the sobbing, snotty nosed, make-up running down my face kind of crying. I walked into my room. With my clothes on I climbed into my bed and pulled the covers over my head. I was sobbing

and crying saying, "I can't do this. I can't do this."
Eventually I stopped crying, dragged myself out of the
bed, combed my hair, fixed my makeup, and went on
my date.

A few days later I mentioned my behavior to my
singles pastor, and he said, "Julie, don't you remember
in school learning about positive stress? It can be just
as stressful as negative stress." "Oh yeah, but I only
know how to manage negative stress." That was a
wakeup call for me. All my energy had gone towards
my survival and getting out of a bad situation. I did
not have the skills to manage positive stress.

Once I learned what my stressors were, I learned
how to manage the positive stress. Thoughts are very
powerful. Sometimes we believe we are not prepared
to cope with new or different situations. It is important
to decide what matters most. At first, I saw my new,
healthy relationship as overwhelming and stressful. I
had a physical reaction to the changes that were
occurring in my life. I wanted to "flee." Instead, I
reached out to a trusted friend who offered me
guidance. I changed my thinking and interpretation of
the stress, and I decided being in a healthy relationship
was something I wanted. I learned how to identify and
manage the stressors in my life and changed my
reaction to the stress.

A stressor is anything that causes the release of
stress hormones. There are two broad categories of
stressors: physiological stressors and psychological
stressors. Things that cause stress are stressors, and

stress is a personal reaction to a stressor.

Here are some things that can cause the release of stress hormones:

- Money problems.
- Marital problems.
- Divorce.
- Being a single parent.
- Health problems.
- Workplace environment.
- Death in the family.
- Raising children.
- Job loss.
- Getting married.

Some effects of stress are:
- Overeating.
- Undereating.
- Alcohol abuse.
- Using drugs to self-medicate.
- Increased cigarette smoking.
- Crying more than usual.
- Angry outbursts.
- More accidents.
- More illnesses.
- Withdrawing from friends and family.

- Relationship problems.
- Allergies.
- Asthma attacks.
- Menstrual problems.
- Over sleeping.
- Feeling insecure.
- Low self-esteem.

How to reduce stress:

- Exercise. This reduces stress and has a terrific effect on people both mentally and physically. Go for a walk, run, or work out on a regular basis.
- Reach out to people. Call a friend, write a letter, or invite someone to walk and talk with you.
- Reduce your chores. Make them into smaller chores. You do not have to accomplish everything in a day. Recruit others to help you out. Divide up chores within the family.
- If you drink a lot of caffeine, cut it back. Caffeine stays in your system for many hours after being consumed.
- Know your personal boundaries. Don't say yes to everything. Take a pass on some things.
- Take personal breaks throughout the day. Read a book, sip some tea, or do some gardening. Get involved in something that inspires you.

- Eliminate the use of illegal drugs and avoid excessive alcohol consumption.
- Eat a healthy and balanced diet full of fruits, vegetables, and proteins.
- Deep breathe. Breathe all the way down into your gut. This slows down your nervous system and helps you relax.
- Talk openly and honestly. Align your head, heart, and gut, and say it like you mean it.
- Get counseling or see a medical professional if you are unable to reduce your stress on your own.
- Participate in relaxation techniques like massages, yoga, or meditation.
- Laugh whenever and wherever you can.
- Consider getting a pet. Pets help some people reduce their stress.
- Most importantly be yourself. Be the best you-you can be!

What will you commit to doing differently to reduce your stress? List some things you are willing to change and work on.

- _____
- _____
- _____

You will never be able to control another person. You can only control yourself and your own behavior. Because of this, it's best to invest energy into something you can control, and that is you.

When everything feels out of control that is when people try to control the impossible. Remember, you will never be able to control other people. There are things in this world you will not ever be able to change. There will always be 24 hours in a day. Holidays will always come and go. Children grow up and move on. You can't change the way you were raised. Controlling how others drive isn't going to happen. You will never be able to control your teenager's mood swings or your two year old's tantrums. People dying, loved ones getting terminally ill, and tragic accidents are out of your control. Don't waste your energy even trying to control these things, because you will never succeed.

There are many things, however, that you can be in control of. Deciding how to treat others is up to you. What kind of self-care you will participate in is up to you. Will you exercise? Will you eat healthy? Will you reduce your to-do list? Will you make goals for yourself? What values will you instill in your children? Will you choose friends who add joy to your life?

I believe everyone has a legacy. A legacy is not only for the rich and famous. If I were to take a panoramic picture of you and your community, then lay it out for viewing, what would people say about you?  Would they say, "Oh my, she is so grouchy" or "Approach her cautiously because you never know if she is in a good mood or a bad mood." Or would they say, "She is the friendliest person, so supportive and she has such a positive attitude." Whether you believe it or not, you create your legacy, and everyone has one. Are you satisfied with your legacy?  If not what changes will you be willing to make and how will you make those changes?

My legacy now is:

_____

_____

Do I need or want to change it?

_____

_____

If yes, write down how you will begin to make changes to your legacy.  Here are a few suggested changes you could make.  Perhaps try volunteering on a project with a smile on your face.  You may wish to bring treats to your next meeting without being asked. You could try listening to people talk without interrupting them.  Those are just a few possible suggestions.

List below some changes you are willing to make:

_____

_____

_____

_____

_____

_____

_____

_____

_____

_____

_____

_____

Here are some things to understand about PTSD. According to the Diagnostic and Statistical Manual of Mental Disorders (DSM-5) published by the American Psychiatric Association (APA), Post-Traumatic Stress Disorder (PTSD) is a mental health disorder. The person with PTSD has been exposed to a traumatic event in which both of the following were present:

- The person experienced, witnessed, or was confronted with an event or events that involved actual or threatened death or serious injury, or a threat to the physical integrity of self or others.
- The person's response involved intense fear, helplessness, or horror.

Most people think about war veterans when they talk about PTSD. Anyone can be diagnosed with PTSD because it occurs following life-threatening events. Natural disasters, terrorist incidents, domestic violence, serious accidents, child abuse, sexual assault, or witnessing a life threatening event can cause PTSD.

According to the Mayo Clinic "It can affect people from age three until their death. It can last for weeks, months, years, or a lifetime. It requires a medical diagnosis because it is a psychiatric disorder."

Therapy for PTSD often involves several different types of treatment. A medical doctor may prescribe medications to manage stress, anxiety, panic attacks, and depression. Cognitive Behavioral Therapy has shown to be a very effective type of counseling for PTSD. Many people benefit from talking about their trauma with others who have had similar experiences and therefore prefer group therapy. Eye Movement Desensitization and Reprocessing (EMDR) is a highly successful mode of treatment used with people who have been diagnosed with PTSD.

Here are numerous possible symptoms of PTSD:

- Crying frequently.
- Nightmares.
- Confusion.
- Flashbacks.
- Always watchful and hyper alert.
- Panic attacks.
- Out of control emotions.
- Easily angered.
- Inability to relax and feel safe.
- Nervousness and being really jumpy.
- Disruptive sleep, cannot fall asleep, cannot stay asleep.
- Waking up drenched in sweat.
- Isolated from others.
- Suicidal thoughts.
- Feeling like a person going crazy.
- Uncomfortable in crowds.

If you believe you are suffering from PTSD, seek treatment as soon as possible. There is help out there for you. If left untreated, PTSD can cause problems in your health, relationships, job, parenting, or marriage.

I am encouraging you to work through your issues with the help of good professionals. They really do want to help you. Find a good support group. It is important to understand that you are not the only person who has gone through traumatic events. The more you talk in a safe environment, the more the symptoms of PTSD are likely to be greatly reduced.

Sometimes family members are invited into therapy, so everyone can learn how to cope with PTSD as an emotionally healthy and supportive unit. PTSD is a psychiatric disorder. Get the help you deserve.

# Chapter 10

## University Bound

Before Jeffrey's 4<sup>th</sup> birthday, a two bedroom Housing and Urban Development (HUD) townhouse apartment became vacant, and we were invited to move in. My welfare grant had gone up, and my rent was adjusted to $123 including utilities. We each had our own bedroom upstairs with a living-room, dining area, and kitchen downstairs. It was more space than we were accustomed to, and we loved it.

We packed up our belongings, and with the help of friends and neighbors moved to our new home. From my front door I could see the apartment playground. This allowed Jeffrey to play independently while being properly supervised. It was a wonderful place to live and raise a son. I felt comfortable and safe in these apartments.

By now I was attending California State University, Sacramento (CSUS) studying Criminal Justice and Psychology. My major was Criminal Justice, but I wanted to learn everything I could about human behavior. I was determined to never be abused again.

By my third semester at CSUS, I wanted to write about joint custody, a new idea in the family court system at the time. I asked my Criminal Justice adviser, Dr. Walker, if I could use this topic for a report, and he approved. I also asked my professor in the Psychology Department if I could get Psychology credit. Dr. Kiley, my psychology professor, said she would approve if I added a psychological perspective to my report. She also suggested I interview a large sample group with specific questions about their personal experience with joint custody and the court system.

Dr. Kiley introduced me to Paul Lawson, a graduate student in the Psychology Department. Paul was majoring in Applied Psychology. As part of Paul's final project for his Master's Degree, he was going to help me gather and compile data, then put the numbers together so I could write my report.

Paul was a personable and handsome man about seven years older than me. He was divorced and had one son who visited him every weekend. His grades were straight A's, and his knowledge of statistics was amazing. He drove a nice little pickup truck and owned a mobile home in West Sacramento. Paul had three siblings, and his parents had been married for over 40 years. Their home was located in Carmichael after they moved from their 40 acre ranch in the Auburn area. On paper Paul looked great.

As we worked on the project, we talked about everything under the sun. I was actually having fun with our long conversations. It seemed like we had so much in common. Education and family were important to both of us. Eventually, we began going out on dates. I met his son and parents, and they seemed very nice. Paul never made a pass at me. He was a perfect gentleman. This was a much needed change for me.

Every school day Paul parked at his sister's house and walked to the campus. He wanted the exercise and the free parking. My son was still enrolled in the CSUS Childcare Center. After school I walked to the center to pick him up. One rainy evening Paul, who always had an umbrella when it rained, asked if he could walk me to my car. He offered to share his umbrella so I would stay dry.

We had been seeing each other and working together on the report for about two months. We were becoming very close, and he continued to be a perfect gentleman. I accepted his offer, and we walked out to get my car. I asked him if he wanted a ride over to his sister's house, and he said yes. Together we drove over to the Childcare Center to get Jeffrey. Paul went inside the center with me, and I felt great having a cute guy beside me.

When we walked back to my car in the pouring rain, Jimmy came charging at me from out of nowhere. He was yelling, "I want my boy. Give me my boy!" This was so shocking! After our court date, Jimmy had moved back to Tennessee. I loved having him far away from me because it made me feel safe. I had let my guard down. When I saw Jimmy, I couldn't catch my breath. I couldn't think, and I panicked. I froze in place, and then I started crying uncontrollably. Paul surprised me by becoming very protective. He put himself between me and Jimmy. He told me to get in the car. Then he pointed his umbrella at Jimmy and told him, "Get back and leave them alone."

I jumped in my car, started up the engine, and Paul got in. He told me to drive away. As I drove I looked in my rear view mirror. I could see Jimmy standing there in the cold, pouring rain. I felt sorry for him for a moment, then I remembered Jimmy had found me on a large university campus and had a history of hurting me. He was back in town, and my world was again about to be turned upside down. I dropped Paul off at his sister's house. As he exited my car he said, "Don't worry the Bible says we must take care of the widows and orphans. I won't let anything happen to you. You're safe with me."

The next month was torture. Jimmy found out where my classes on campus were located. I came out of a Criminal Justice class, and he was in the hall talking and laughing with students. I would quickly run to the Psychology Department and hide in a private room for honor students called the Psi Chi Room. I was an honor student. Yes, you read that right, and I could use the Psi Chi room any time. Paul hung out in this room too, so I felt safe.

There was a Jimboy's Taco fast food restaurant located on the corner of the street where we lived. The bathroom was on the backside of the building. Jimmy figured out we lived in that general area and started sleeping in that bathroom at night. He walked the neighborhoods at night looking for my car and apartment. He had seen my car at the Childcare Center and knew I was driving a dark blue Volkswagen Bug. Eventually, the owner of Jimboy's called the sheriff, and Jimmy was removed from their property. The sheriff called to notify me because I had an Order of Protection against Jimmy. It frightened me to know he was looking for Jeffrey and me and that he was looking so close to where we lived.

Paul and I continued to work on my report and continued to date and get to know each other better. Jeffrey and Paul's son got along well, and we did things together on the weekends. Paul's parents seemed to like me, and we visited them often. I felt safe with these new people in my life. Things were feeling normal again.

After a few months, Jeffrey and I moved into Paul's mobile home. Jimmy was still stalking me, and I was more frightened than ever. I knew what he was capable of doing to me when he wasn't provoked, and now that I had moved on, he was even furious and agitated than before.

Almost a year after we met, Paul and I got married in the living room of the mobile home. We invited one other family, our friend and college schoolmate Shirley, her husband, and their two sons. John, a man who also attended CSUS, performed the wedding ceremony. Paul planned the entire event, including the food and music. He thought it best if we did not invite our families. I was so caught up in the excitement of my life turning in a better direction that I went along with this crazy plan.

When I told my mom I was married and had moved to West Sacramento, she was shocked and disappointed. However, she decided to throw us a reception. She did not know Paul well at all and wanted to give him the benefit of the doubt. We invited many of our friends from school. Mom and Dennis were very impressed with our friends. I believe meeting all these wonderful and fun people put them at ease. They were happy that I was hanging around with smart, educated, funny, and very nice people. Looking back, I believe they felt I was safe and they didn't have to worry as much about Jeffrey and me.

Unfortunately, the peace did not last for Mom, for Dennis, or for me. Paul was dual diagnosed with a mental illness and a drug addiction by a psychiatrist. Back then I knew very little about mental illness. Paul self-medicated with illegal street drugs because he did not like how his prescription medications made him feel. When he was off his medications, Paul lapsed into intense manic episodes. He would not sleep. Sometimes he would go without sleep for up to 72 hours. Then when he wanted or needed to sleep, he would take street drugs to bring himself down, and he would sleep extensively over the next few days.

There were many things about Paul that I did not know until after I had married him. He had been discharged from the United States Navy due to his mental health issues. Paul had been in and out of psychiatric hospitals for years. He had even undergone Electroconvulsive Therapy (ECT).

After Paul and I married, I found out he was losing his mobile home for nonpayment, and his college grades were either all A's or all F's depending on when and if he was taking his prescribed medications. He really had very little relationships with his parents or siblings. His mother said to me once after Paul and I were married, "He's all yours. You can take care of him now." Paul had looked good on paper, and I thought we were a good match. I believed we both valued education, had strong work ethics, and were close to our families. I had been completely unaware of all of Paul's serious mental health and drug problems.

Before Paul completely lost his mobile home, my mom, who was a real estate broker, stepped in and helped him sell it for a small profit. After the sale, we moved into a crappy apartment in Broderick near the Sacramento River. We lived there for a year. During that time, Paul was in and out of a psychiatric hospital in Woodland, and I was drained emotionally and physically. I was learning his hospitalizations coincided with his use of street drugs. Paul told me he loved being in the hospital because he felt it was relaxing, and he felt no pressures.

Paul was extremely emotionally abusive. His words were hurtful. He was rough on Jeffrey, making rules that were impossible for a child to follow. He threw our Christmas tree out in the yard one year because "Christmas was a pagan holiday." He did not want us to do things with my family. Our life was again getting very crazy.

One day while reading a local newspaper, I found a small two bedroom house in the Rio Linda area for sale by owner for $33,000. The owner wanted nothing down and agreed to carry the loan. The house payment would be $180 a month. By now I worked at a group home and had my own money. I called the number in the newspaper, and the owners wanted to meet me and my son. I was thankful that they liked me and Jeffrey and agreed to sell me their little house. I gave them my first house payment at their kitchen table, signed a one page contract, we shook hands, and we had a new place to live.

I called my mom to tell her the exciting news. Mom was not impressed or happy with my house buying experience. In fact she was very angry. Mom wanted to know what school district Jeffrey would be in. She wanted to know if I had the well and septic tank checked out. She asked all sorts of other questions about the roof, the heater, and everything else home buyers needed to be concerned about. I had no answers and felt really dumb. My family had no idea about the downward turn my life had again taken. I was embarrassed to let anyone know, and I believed buying this little house was a perfect way out of this emotionally abusive life I was living in.

Paul found out I bought a house and told me

very loudly that we were married, and we would all be moving into that house. My heart sunk. I was not going to be free after all. We all moved into the cute little house. Paul was taking his prescription medication and working with his doctor. For a while, life calmed down and things were fairly smooth. The home came with a large plot of ground. Paul loved to garden and planted lots of flowers and vegetables. The calm did not last. Eventually, Paul went off his prescription medications and started self-medicating again with illegal street drugs.

As I mentioned earlier, I knew very little about mental illness and even less about drug addiction. Paul never told me he was using illegal drugs, and I assumed his prescription medications were not working properly. Together we visited his psychiatrist and tried to get the medications prescribed properly. Paul always blamed the psychiatrist, and I believed it was the psychiatrist's fault things were off-kilter in our home. I had no idea he was not taking his medications as prescribed.

Because of his numerous hospitalizations, Paul finally decided it would be in his best interest to sign up with the California Department of Rehabilitation Services. He was assigned to a Rehabilitation Counselor who enrolled Paul into their Job Services Program. Since he had completed his Master's Degree in Applied Psychology, he was placed for job training with the U.S. Department of Agriculture (USDA) in Davis as a Statistician. The USDA eventually hired

Paul as a full time permanent employee. At about the same time, Yolo County Department of Social Services hired me and stationed me in Davis. It was perfect. We had one car, and we carpooled together. I found great childcare in our neighborhood for Jeffrey close by the grammar school. Things were looking more promising.

I started a career in a field I knew and loved. I got sick leave, vacation time, paid holidays, medical benefits, and retirement. My dad was a Sacramento County employee. I was familiar with government employment and was happy to follow in his footsteps. I could support myself and Jeffrey if need be.

The peace and stability did not last long. Paul continued to tweak his medications and lie about his behavior. He continued to be emotionally abusive, and he was also becoming more agitated and aggressive. Paul's mother was keeping Paul's son on all the weekend visitations saying she feared for her grandson's emotional safety. Things were getting more horrible by the day, and Jeffrey, now a third grader, was becoming more reclusive and was spending more time alone in his room.

During my first year working for Yolo County, we went on strike. I didn't know much about strikes, but I learned fast. First, don't cross the picket line and second, you only get $25 a week from the union. I was shocked. How would I ever live on $100 a month? Yolo County employee strikes could go on for months. I was a very new Yolo County employee.

I had only recently left my job with Guadalupe Group Homes, so I called them and asked if I could come back and work for them until the strike ended. They gladly agreed, and I worked for the group home until the strike ended. I never missed a paycheck.

My shift at the group home was from Monday evening until Wednesday morning. I slept at the group home Monday and Tuesday nights while I took care of 13 boys who were in the probation system. The money was good, and I got my 40 hour work week done in two days. That allowed me to be home the rest of the week with my son. Paul and the babysitter took care of Jeffrey while I was working

This seemed like a good fix that kept me financially afloat. One Tuesday night I got a desperate emergency call from Paul. He was yelling hysterically into the phone, "That crazy drunk ex of yours just hit me in the nose and took your damn kid!" I didn't know what Paul was talking about because to my knowledge Jimmy had gone back to Tennessee months ago, and I thought he had no idea where we lived.

I was completely unaware that Paul and Jimmy had been talking on the phone for the past several months. Jimmy returned to California with his younger half-brother and wanted to see Jeffrey. He called Paul who invited him to our house for a visit. Jimmy was drunk and said, "I want my wife and son back." Paul and Jimmy argued, and Jeffrey was snatched again and put into Jimmy's vehicle, and they drove off. Paul did not call the police. He called me.

The only thing I knew for sure was my son was gone, and his father had taken him again. I called my boss to tell him I had an emergency and had to leave. While waiting for my replacement to come and relieve me, the phone rang and it was Jeffrey calling from a pay phone. "Hi Mom," he said in a cheerful voice. "Where are you?" "At the Circle K." "What Circle K?" "I'm not sure." "Let me talk to your Dad." "He's not here." "What do you mean he's not here? It is 10:30 at night." "The police took him." "Who are you there with?" "My uncle." I felt a sense of relief thinking he was with his Uncle Lawrence who I knew would not let anything happen to my son. "Let me talk to Uncle Lawrence." "He's not here." "Which uncle are you with then?" "Uncle Bob." "Who the hell is Uncle Bob?" "My dad's little brother. He's really cool." "Put him on the phone, now."

A young man who I had never met or even heard of before got on the phone. I was furious and unloaded my anger on him. Bob had only been in California for two days and did not have a clue where he was. He was 16 years old and scared. Jimmy had driven to the Circle K to buy more beer. The store clerk realized he was drunk and refused to sell beer to him. The boys got out of the car when Jimmy started arguing with the clerk. He became belligerent, and the store clerk called the police. Jimmy was arrested and was taken to jail.

The Sacramento City police left these two boys

114

on the sidewalk. Maybe the police did not realize the boys were with Jimmy. I didn't know the whole story. All I knew was my son was alone without adult supervision on the sidewalk outside a Circle K at 10:30 p.m., and I was furious.

I rushed over to the Circle K on Auburn Boulevard, a street known for prostitution and drug sales. When I pulled up I saw two kids, a 3rd grader and another who should have been a 10th grader huddled together by the pay phone. When Jeffrey saw my little truck pull up, he ran into my arms. I told him to get in the truck, glad I found him safe and sound.

I was getting ready to pull away and looked over at Bob who looked terrified. I wanted nothing more to do with any of this family, but I could not leave this child there on the sidewalk alone. I got out of the car and used the pay phone to call Jimmy's sister, Glenda. She agreed to pick up Bob. We all waited in my truck until she arrived, and I told Bob to go with her. I did not speak to the sister and never saw Bob again.

Jeffrey and I did not talk on our ride back to our house. I did not know what to say. I always felt guilty that Jimmy was my son's father. I would have given anything for Jeffrey to have a different and better dad. I also felt guilty because Paul, the stepfather, was nearly as bad. Physical abuse is horrible, but when someone hits you with his fist you can rationally say to yourself "Your fist hit my face, and that is terrible." Emotional abuse is trickier because the abuser can make you believe you really are all those terrible things

115

the abuser is saying about you.

Paul was messing with his medications, using illegal drugs, cheating with other women, and had been in cahoots with Jimmy for months. I was furious with him, and he knew it. I had to get out of another terrible situation and the sooner the better.

The strike at Yolo County ended sooner than expected. I spent the next three months in Medi-Cal training. Life at home seemed to calm down a little, and Jeffrey loved his babysitter who even made us dinner several times a week. After my Medi-Cal training was over, I was permanently stationed at the Davis office. Paul and I continued to carpool.

Paul became more agitated and was becoming very aggressive with his words and behaviors towards both Jeffrey and me. He did not physically hit either one of us, but he did grab our arms tightly and roughly to get us to comply with his demands. We grew to hate him. He was not a very nice person. I did not feel physically trapped, but emotionally I allowed myself to feel trapped. I still had not told my family how horrible our home life was.

Over one weekend I was thinking about my life. I was married to Jimmy for two years and nine months. My third anniversary to Paul was three months away. Nothing was peaceful or fun about being married to Paul. It was hectic and unstable. In early December, I was starting to make plans for the holidays. I was thinking about the previous year when Paul threw our Christmas tree out into the yard. I remembered how Jeffrey and I put the Christmas tree back up in his room and celebrated quietly together on his bunkbed. These were not happy holiday memories. Right then I decided I was no longer going to live in a crazy lifestyle, and there was no way I was going to have a third year anniversary with Paul.

The following Monday morning, I carpooled to work with Paul as usual. Then I went to work and asked my boss for the rest of the day off. I explained I had a family emergency that needed to be resolved. She approved my leave, and I drove home. I called my mother and explained my entire situation. Mom called Dennis at work, and they both agreed that Jeffrey and I would move home with them for awhile. I spent the day packing up my most important belongings to take with me. I moved some of them to a friend's empty spare bedroom because of limited space at Mom's house. At 3:30 p.m. I drove the pickup truck back to Davis and parked it in the USDA parking lot. Then I placed a note on the steering wheel that read, "Take yourself home. I have my own ride." A friend had followed me out there and then drove me back to pick up Jeffrey from childcare. That evening we were living with my mom and Dennis.

Jeffrey stayed in his same school for the rest of the school year. Every morning I dropped him off at the babysitter's house, and after work I picked him up. We stayed at my mom's house from November until the end of the school year in June. I made the decision to pay a small amount of rent and pay for the electric bill and the natural gas bill. I wanted to contribute at least something to my own upkeep. I wanted and needed to feel empowered.

I learned the hard way that finding a guy who looked nearly perfect on paper was not enough for a good relationship or a good marriage. I also learned that I was not really the victim, but I had to admit I contributed to many of my own problems by trusting too quickly and too easily. I still had so much to learn.

# Chapter 11

# Relaunched

Jeffrey and I stayed with Mom and Dennis until I felt safe enough physically and emotionally to leave once and for all. Mom said I needed family support, and I needed to go home and get relaunched properly into the world. In my mind, I thought it would take about two weeks. In reality, we lived with my family for seven months.

Jeffrey never asked why we were living with his grandparents and not going back to our house. Once he said, "What about the rest of my toys?" I told him he'd get new toys for Christmas, and that was the end of that. He was as glad as I was to get out of that terrible emotionally abusive relationship.

Dennis was born and raised in Minnesota and brought his Midwest values to our family. We ate dinner every night together as a family. We talked about our day and visited with each other. It was relaxing and fun. One Sunday night Dennis opened his wallet and handed Jeffrey five dollars and said, "Here's your allowance. You can spend it on anything you want." Jeffrey was shocked, surprised, and then he got the biggest smile on his face. It was a smile I had not seen for a long time. His happiness and excitement brought tears to my eyes. Dennis then pulled out a 20 dollar bill, handed it to me, and said, "Here's your allowance. You can spend it on anything you want, except bills."

Dennis knew Paul had opened more than 10 credit cards in my name and maxed them out. In addition, there were medical bills I was personally responsible for due to an earlier gallbladder surgery. I had Blue Cross insurance but did not understand how a deductible worked. I soon learned 80 percent coverage meant I was responsible for the other 20 percent. Needless to say I had no money to spare. When Dennis gave me that 20 dollars, it felt like a 100 dollars in cash and a 1,000,000 dollars in love.

Dennis gave us our allowances every Sunday night for the entire seven months we lived with them. It was strange to me. I paid them a small amount for rent and paid for the gas and electric bills. Dennis then gave me 80 dollars a month back in allowance. I truly did not understand this act of kindness.

One night over dinner I shared my confusion. I am not exactly sure what I said, probably something like, "Why do you do this? It's so silly. I pay you, then you pay me." Within about a second of me finishing my sentence, his Midwestern temper came out, and his voice was loud and sharp. "You are not a second class citizen. No matter what anyone has tried to convince you of, Julie, you are first class!" His tone of voice scared me, and I started to cry. Dennis came over and took me in his arms and let me cry and sob until I was completely cried out. Then he said, "Don't let anyone ever again treat you like a second class citizen. You are first class all the way, and don't you ever forget it." From that day forward, my stepdad Dennis was in my corner. I knew his kindness was real and had no strings attached. His love for me was real, and he always wanted the best for me and Jeffrey. I adored my stepdad until the moment he passed away in the family home years later.

I knew deep down I needed to stay with my family until I felt physically and emotionally strong enough to venture out on my own. Coming home with a child after living with two abusive husbands was not something I was proud of. I was embarrassed and ashamed. I belittled myself and complained to my mom about the mess I had made of my life. Mom would just smile and say, "You needed to come home and get properly relaunched." One day I looked up the meaning of relaunched. It means "To start something again and hope that it will be more successful than before." Mom was right. I very much needed to come home and get relaunched.

Before Jeffrey's third grade school year ended, I began looking for a nice and affordable place to live. Over the seven months, my emotional and physical strength grew strong. I felt calm, confident, capable, and free. I was earning enough money to pay down my bills and was nearly debt free. As much as I loved living with my family, I knew it was time for us to move out on our own. I was determined to have a successful life. I never again wanted to be a burden on my family or cause them to worry about my safety. I wanted to make it on my own. I told my mom, "One day I will make you proud!" Mom said, "Julie, I already am proud of you."

The weekend after Jeffrey finished third grade, we moved into our own apartment in Sacramento just on the border of Carmichael. I chose this apartment because it was affordable, large, had two bedrooms, and was next to the local YMCA which had a large grassy greenbelt area beside it. There was no play structure, but Jeffrey had lots of grassy areas where he could use his imagination and play whatever games he could dream up.

During the summer, I used the YMCA for my daily childcare provider. Jeffrey loved the YMCA and wanted to go on the week long summer camping trips. Jimmy did not pay child support, and there wasn't any extra money. The weeks Jeffrey went to camp, I worked night shifts at the group home to pay for the next session of summer camp. Mom and Dennis would have gladly paid for summer camp, but I was determined to make it on my own and not be a burden to others. My county job was going well. I was in therapy, and I attended a support group. We found a home church. Jeffrey's grades and behavior were great, and we were both feeling happy, safe, and calm. We lived in our apartment for two years, through his fourth and fifth grades.

At the end of Jeffrey's fifth grade, my godmother Thelma called me up and said, "The pink house is going to be empty at the end of the month. Do you want to rent it?" The pink house was built for Thelma's mother and was located on Thelma and her husband Lewis's property. After her mother's death, the house had been used as a rental. Thelma's daughter Luann lived there years before when Jeffrey was a baby. He was used to spending time in this house. It was a win-win situation. I asked about the cost of the rent. Thelma said, "We get $500 for rent." My heart sank. My apartment rented for $325, and I was surviving perfectly. Spending an additional $175 would push my budget to the max. Plus, I had the YMCA daycare and the grassy greenbelt for a play area.

Thelma said she'd babysit Jeffrey after school. Both homes were on the same property, and after school he could walk to her house for a snack and do his homework. He could stay there until I got home from work. I worked 43 miles away with a one hour commute. It felt safer to have someone who cared about us watching him, especially with me working so far away.

I agreed to move in, but I needed to have some surgery first. My mom was very excited that we would be moving back to Fair Oaks closer to family. I gave notice on my apartment, had my surgery, and during my recovery Mom negotiated with my godparents to allow her and Dennis to fix the place up before we moved in. The pink house was old and very dated. Thelma and Lewis were reluctant for any changes to be made, but mom was relentless with her negotiations and eventually they agreed.

Mom and Dennis scraped wallpaper off and then painted the walls. They installed a new bathroom vanity, replaced kitchen countertops, bought and hung new blinds and mirrors, installed new light fixtures, and replaced the kitchen cabinet knobs. They hired a woman to hang a wallpaper trim around the kitchen and dining room area. Thelma was so impressed with how hard Mom and Dennis worked, she paid to have new carpeting installed. By the time Jeffrey and I moved into the pink house, it looked like a new home. I asked Mom why she worked so hard and spent so much money, and she said, "It's the final phase of your relaunching."

I continued to be involved in my church and loved attending the singles group. Jeffrey came with me because they had childcare in an adjacent room. Every Tuesday night we had fellowship, singing, and a lesson. It felt like youth group for adults. Most of the people who attended were quite a bit older than me, so it felt safe and fun. We went camping a couple times a year, dancing once a month, had potlucks for every holiday, and most people had kids, so there were lots of family activities. I attended the singles group for several more years.

One day I decided it was time for me to hang out with people my own age and start dating again. I had invested time and energy into improving my thinking, and I no longer felt like a second class citizen. I learned how to trust my head, heart, and gut. I was clear about my code of conduct. I was getting promoted in my job which meant more income, and I was completely out of debt. I had a savings account. I was happy in my home. I made new emotionally healthy friends, and I was recovering from domestic abuse because of my strong support system and my own determination. I was a grown woman and put effort into being a good mother. I had a strong, loud, and proud voice. I was no longer a victim without a voice.

On what I thought was my last night of singles group, I said a silent prayer for myself and my future. I asked God for guidance, wisdom, and understanding to do his will. Fifteen minutes later when I walked into the room, I met a man named Tom. He was a newcomer to our singles group. He was cute, and I loved talking to him. He was funny, thoughtful, very smart, and one of the kindest men I had ever met. Wow! I asked myself, "How could this be happening?" Needless to say, I didn't leave singles group until Tom and I got married in the church two years later.

# Chapter 12

## Improving Your Emotional Health

After everything has been lost, you are still you. No matter what you think, you will impact others. There are gifts from where you have come from. I wrote this book because I wanted to be useful to others. At one time I had lost everything, my pride, my friendships, my dream of a good marriage, close ties with my family, my education, my clothing, my household goods, my innocence, and the most important thing, my son Jeffrey.

I was bound and determined to never give up. I was fighting for our lives. Food, clothing, shelter, and our personal safety were at the top of my list of needs. With no money, no job, and basically no clue of what I needed and wanted to be doing, I wasn't sure how I was going to get out of and stay out of the mess I was in. Being a victim of domestic violence was not the life for me.

I have led most of my life with my heart. I trust too easily and want to believe what most people are telling me. That has not always served me well. Learning who to trust and when to trust does not happen automatically. First you have to learn how to trust yourself. Increasing your self-esteem, self-worth, and interpersonal skills is a must.

126

I did not want my heart to become hardened, cold, or mean. The wonderful families who influenced my life when I was a child supported my belief that many people were kind and loving. I knew there were good people in this world, and I was determined to find them. I heard a teacher once say, "People grow into the conversations around them." I went looking for those positive conversations that would add to my life instead of taking away from it. I made it my personal mission to learn how to increase my self-esteem, my self-worth, and my interpersonal skills. I didn't have any idea where to start, so I began by looking deep within myself.

Trusting Yourself

Living in an abusive relationship can dull your gut reactions to things. It can become nearly impossible to make good decisions for yourself. You may have been told over and over again that there is nothing to be afraid of, or to quit acting depressed, or don't you dare raise your voice. Over time gut reactions become an untrustworthy emotion. You talk yourself out of what you are truly feeling.

These are the feelings you need to recognize:

- Fears: Unpleasant emotions caused by the belief that someone or something is dangerous, likely to cause pain, or is a threat.

- Depression: Feeling sad, hopeless, and unimportant for a length of time.
- Resentment: Feelings when you have been treated unfairly.
- Anger: Strong feelings of annoyance, displeasure, or hostility.

It is important to pay attention to emotions. This includes the good, the bad, and the ugly. Many abused women do not allow themselves to feel their emotions, especially their feelings of anger. They have already been victims of another person's anger and were hurt badly physically and emotionally. Often times there is a fear of becoming angry because it might trigger an increase in the abuser's own anger, causing him to seriously harm or even kill the abused woman or other loved ones. Keeping feelings stable, not too low and not too high, feels like the safest course of action.

## Core Values

Having core values, or a code of conduct, is important. Core values give us a structure for living and making decisions. I have a few core values I try to live by most of the time. Notice I said "try" and "most of the time." I am not a perfect person. I am always a work in progress, and I mess up. That is part of being human. We make mistakes. When I know what my core values are for myself, it's easier to identify what went wrong when I messed up. If I don't have a clue what my core values are, I am lost not knowing in which direction I need to go.

## Julie's Core Values

- I am congruent. My words and my behaviors match.
- I make decisions when my head, my heart, and my gut are aligned. In other words, my head, my heart, and my gut need to be giving me the same message.
- I act like who I hang out with, so I hang out with who I want to act like.
- I give more than I take.
- I strive to have integrity.
- I laugh at myself and my life.
- I am kind to myself and try to be kind to others.

What are your core values? Write down five things that describe who you are and what you stand for. For example, I am polite.

- _____
- _____
- _____
- _____
- _____

Self-talk

How you talk to yourself is very important. We listen to what we say to ourselves whether it is positive or negative. If you are putting yourself down, degrading yourself, or belittling yourself, you will start to believe you are not good enough. The same is true if you exaggerate your accomplishments. If you are telling yourself how great you are all the time, you will begin to wonder if you really are that great. This creates self-doubt and leads to low self-esteem and low self-worth. Instead, look for some middle ground that accurately describes your best self. Remember you are a valuable person and have much to offer to the world. Learn how to be your own very best friend. Treat yourself as you would a best friend. In your self-talk, be kind, generous, loving, and find things to laugh about. This will help increase your self-esteem and self-worth.

Only you can boost your self-worth. Quit trying

to figure out what everyone else is saying and thinking about you.  Develop and work on strengthening your own personality.  Be the best you - you can be!

## Unhealthy Crutches

It is impossible to give yourself healthy love when you are hiding behind addictions.  Being addicted to drugs, alcohol, pornography, gambling, the internet, food, exercise, or sex is a clear sign you are not dealing with your personal issues.

I have used food as a crutch since I was a young child.  We use crutches because they work.  Actually, they work until they no longer work.  Let me explain.  Food comforted me for years.  If I felt sad, scared, lonely, bored, or mad, I found a particular food to eat.  Each emotion seemed to need either a salty, crunchy, sour, or sweet treat.  I ate and felt great for a few moments.  Then I felt stuffed, bloated, guilty, sad, and mad.  I had an unhealthy addictive relationship with food.

I knew I had to make changes, so I worked to improve my self-esteem and self-worth.  The mentally healthier I got, the less I used food as a coping mechanism.  Then my mom died in 2014, and I went back to my old habits and the unhealthy crutch of eating to suppress my feelings.  The difference is, this time it did not work.  I gained 30 pounds and never once suppressed a feeling.  I realized since I knew better, I had to do better.  I had to deal with my feelings and work the steps that originally got my self-

131

esteem and self-worth raised in the first place. I am a work in progress, and working on my self-esteem is an ongoing process that is never done.

What are your emotional crutches? How do you use your crutches?

_____

_____

_____

_____

_____

_____

_____

_____

_____

_____

_____

_____

## Gut Reactions

We hear people all the time say they've had a gut reaction about this or that. What really is a gut reaction? According to the dictionary, gut reaction is a noun and means, "A reaction to a situation derived from a person's instinct and experience."

I believe it is important to learn to accurately listen to your gut reactions. Don't make decisions just because you should, could, ought to, or are supposed to. The words should, could, ought to, and supposed to are poison words. Give yourself permission to purge these words from your vocabulary. They do nothing but impose guilt, shame, anxiety, and confusion on your decision making. Throw them away! Learn to listen to yourself as you analyze the pros and cons when you are trying to solve problems.

Make decisions because they feel right and work best for you. Don't make decisions because they work best for everyone else. It is impossible to have high self-esteem and self-worth when you allow everyone else to make all your decisions for you.

Learn how to trust your gut. At first it will feel strange because you may not be used to making real decisions for yourself. You might feel more comfortable trying to avoid conflict, but in reality you will have more conflict. You will have conflict within yourself, and this will exhaust you.

Trusting your gut is an easy thing to teach and a difficult thing to do. This requires commitment and practice. You also have to trust that you have your

133

best interests at heart. Identify a decision you have been putting off making because it feels too big, too scary, or too complicated. Instead start with something small. What flowers do you want to plant in the spring? What movie do you want to see? What color do you want to paint your bedroom? What day do you want to have friends over for dinner?

Decide what movie you will see this week. Pretend you only have enough time and money for one movie. Think about these questions and write down your answers.

What movie will you see?

_____

Who will you see the movie with, or will you be viewing it alone?

_____

_____

How much money will you spend on the movie?

_____

Will your children be coming, or do you need to hire a babysitter? Who will you hire?

_____

_____

_____

Are you seeing this movie because you really want to see it? Do you just need a break from your life? Is it to spend time with a friend? Are you taking your kids out for a treat?

_____

_____

_____

_____

_____

_____

_____

_____

All those thoughts swirling around in your head about the movie can feel exhausting and overwhelming. Those thoughts can put your mind into overload. Making no decision is easier than making the wrong decision. It's easier to skip the movie altogether than to figure all this out.

Now let's try using your gut reaction. Take a couple of deep breaths, breathing in through your nose and out through your mouth. Relax your whole body. When you are completely relaxed, push your air all the way down to your gut area. Let your air sit down there. It will keep trying to move back up to your heart. It is important to keep deep breathing and pushing your air back into your gut area. Do this until you are able to honestly give yourself the gut reaction to your questions about a movie.

Write down your gut reactions. There are no wrong answers because you can always change your decisions.

_____

_____

_____

_____

_____

_____

In the beginning, searching for your gut reactions will feel uncomfortable. You are not used to putting yourself first, and it may feel a bit selfish. You might be trying to avoid conflict. In reality, it creates more conflict within yourself. Trying to please everyone but yourself can feel emotionally exhausting. You need to learn to trust your gut when you make decisions. Remember, start small. The more you do this the easier it gets.

## Don't Quit

My sister gave me a poem one day when I was feeling low on hope and high on stress. The message in the poem made me believe I could have a better life if I worked at it. It was an affirmation, a positive encouragement that I could hope and work for what I needed. You may have seen a saying on a poster or on the Internet, or heard a song that affects you the same way. We need these affirmations to remind us that we can move forward.

The poem gave me permission to keep going. Only I could make my life better. There was no magic wand. I had to make serious changes to make a better life for myself. There was no room for blaming others. In order to make changes, I could no longer be a victim without a voice.

I wanted to find my own voice. My stress was high, my blood pressure was 230 over 95. My fear of having a stroke was very real. My confidence was low and my hope for making changes was nonexistent. I mistakenly believed everyone else was better than me.

When I worked as a Workshop Facilitator for Yolo County, I learned "Success is not the destiny, but the journey traveled." (Author unknown). The only way to get better was to start on my own personal journey towards recovery. Looking at myself realistically was not going to be fun. This next exercise was a real eye opener for me. I always was clear about the traits I loved in other people, but could not see and believe my own best traits.

Take a few moments to think of a person you admire or respect. Write down that person's name. The person may be living or dead, a family member, friend, or even someone famous.

_____

What five words or traits would you use to describe him or her? Write them down.

- _____

- _____

- _____

- _____

- _____

What five words or traits would you use to describe yourself? Write them down.

- _____

- _____

- _____

- _____

- _____

My hope is the words and traits on each list are similar. People often admire in others what they forget to admire in themselves.

## Positive Thinking

Do you believe you are what you think? Let's test the idea. When you think about uncluttering your personal life by freeing yourself from over-eating, over-spending, over-scheduling, over-stressing, and over-committing, what thoughts come to your mind? If your thoughts are positive, and you get excited about simplifying your personal life, this is because you feel powerful and are expecting positive results. But, if you have thoughts of dread and defeat, it is because you feel powerless and are expecting the results to be negative.

When your thoughts are positive about a particular situation, your feelings will follow in a positive way. The same is true with negative thoughts. If you think negatively, your feelings will follow suit. Most people's thoughts are subconscious. The thoughts are not actually put into words. For example, most people do not say to themselves, "Today I choose to think negatively about myself, and today I choose to be a very unhappy person."

The only way to correct negative thoughts is to learn how to become aware of them. Because thoughts are often subconscious, it is not easy to see the problems. If you don't see the problems, then you won't believe there are problems; therefore, the motivation to change is slim to none.

"People are their own worst enemy." How many times have we heard that, and what does that really even mean? In reality, very few people buy into the idea that our thoughts are powerful. Because of this, gaining control over thoughts, and thinking is not a high priority on to-do lists. Negative thoughts can be an ongoing source of problems for people. Negative thoughts keep people from exploring opportunities that could greatly benefit their lives. The negative thoughts poison relationships, both professionally and personally and also create a victim mentality, which is very emotionally harmful and exhausting.

How does a person become aware of his or her thoughts and then weed out the thoughts that sabotage best intentions? Awareness is critical. Become aware that your thoughts are negative and half the battle is won. You admit there is a need for change.

Get the best information for your situation. Gather information so you have multiple choices when the time comes to make decisions. We make the best decisions when we gather the best information.

Use your best thinking, not just the easiest thinking. Spend time investigating what is really going on. Does your interpretation of the situation match the reality of the situation? Is the person trying to harm you? Are your past thoughts interfering with your current relationship?

Switch your perception of things. Instead of your glass always seeming half empty, start looking at your glass as mostly full. Understanding positive thinking starts with positive self-talk and positive thoughts. The types of unspoken thoughts running through your head will influence how you think. Positive thinking does not mean being unaware of unpleasant situations going on in your world. It merely means you tackle unpleasant things from a more positive position. You have not given up hope that the best outcome could happen.

There are many health benefits when you change from being a negative thinker to a positive thinker. Researchers agree some of these benefits are lower rates of depression, lower levels of stress, increased lifespan, and better psychological and physical well-being.

Becoming a positive thinker will not happen overnight. If you practice being a positive thinker every day, you will cross over into being a positive person. You will learn to be less critical and more accepting. Begin being more positive today. Quit saying "I am not going to get any better at this," and start saying "I will give it another try!"


Making Personal Goals

It is important to set yourself up for success. Most people are real good at making goals and then quitting within six weeks of setting them. Try something different. Make your goals smaller and more manageable. Instead of saying, "I will go to the gym five times this week," revise your goal by saying, "I will go to my gym three times this week and work out for 30 minutes during each visit." You can even get more specific with your goals by naming what will be done at the gym during your visits. Re-framing your goal makes it very clear and helps create feelings of success when your goal is accomplished.

Maybe your goal is to get more sleep. How are you going to make that happen? Just saying it's a goal doesn't make you get more sleep. You need an action plan. Pick a bedtime that feels comfortable, and then start getting ready for bed about 30 minutes before that time. You will need time to change into your pajamas, brush your teeth, and factor in some time to actually fall asleep after your head hits the pillow (usually between 10 and 15 minutes for most people).

If you want to be a more positive person, you have to make an effort to create a positive life. I am here to tell you, merely wishing and hoping you will be a more positive person does not make it happen. Most everyone has days when they are angry, snarky, or grouchy, including me. But if you are negative much more than you are positive in a day, week, or month, then bravo to you for wanting to make the shift. How can you make a shift if you are not in touch with your behavior? You can't! Many people don't think they are really negative even when their friends and family are saying things like, "Now don't be so negative," or "Hear me out before you toss out my idea," or the classic question, "Are you ever positive about anything?"

Personal awareness is the key to making changes. Write your negative comments or negative thoughts down on a piece of paper. Writing them down is the first step towards change. Awareness of the behavior is the second step. You may have been negative for so long that you don't even realize how negative you really are.

Henry Ford said, "Whether you think you can or whether you think you can't, you're right." My hope is that you think you can. After you track your negative comments and thoughts for a day or so, look over the list and pick one negative area you will commit to changing. Maybe it is complaining about your boss, your food server, the traffic, or your significant other. Make a commitment to quit complaining about one thing.

The key is to start small and practice often. Don't expect to be "perfect" because you will never reach the level of perfection. Negativity creeps back in if you're not careful. Replace negative behaviors with positive behaviors. Replace the word can't with can. Replace negative self-talk with positive affirmations.

Remember the childhood story of the little engine that thought he could? He was trying to take his heavy load up a big hill and kept sliding backwards. Each try he'd say, "I think I can, I think I can." Eventually, after several tries, he pulled his heavy load over the mountain. Remember, if you think you can or if you think you can't, you're right. Practicing positive behaviors allows you to be the best you - you can be!

## Improving Your Self-Image

You can always do your best. Your best is never going to be the same from moment to moment. When you wake up refreshed and energized, your best will be better than when you are sick or tired. You don't have to try to do better than your best. Just do your best every day. As you create new habits, your best will get better over time. If you always do your best, it makes it impossible to negatively judge yourself. When you are not negatively judging yourself, you will not suffer from guilt, blame, shame, and self-punishment.

Activities to help you think positively:

- Look in the mirror and focus on the physical attributes you like about yourself. I have a nice smile. I'm warm and friendly. Even as I age, I can still smile and be warm and friendly. Train yourself not to judge your appearance by the way you looked 10 or 20 years ago. Be forward thinking because the past is behind you, and the future is ahead of you.
- Go for a walk because it improves mental health by helping the brain cope with stress. Find a fitness activity that's fun and appeals to you. If you love to dance, then dance. I like to sing and dance while I do karaoke.
- Start a stress journal. Writing things down

145

helps make stress manageable. Feeling overwhelmed? Write down what you are doing, thinking, and feeling. Flip through your journal weekly, and see if you can spot a pattern and determine what is driving your stress.

- Reevaluate your priorities. Have you ever asked yourself, "What's my purpose in life?" or "Am I moving in the right direction?" Maybe you have asked, "What mark do I want to leave on society?" or "What will my legacy be?" On a sheet of paper write down your answers to the above questions.

- Tap into your social network. Maintaining and developing friendships is key. People who are doing things with family and friends at least monthly have reported being significantly happier and had better overall psychological well-being than others who did not have a satisfactory social network. Take a risk and invite someone to coffee, lunch, a movie, or meet someone for a walk and talk in the park.

- Explore new or old passions. Return to some of the favorite activities you've put on hold or try new ones. Drive across the country in an RV, take a cake decorating class, or sign up for the dance class you have always wanted to take but were afraid you wouldn't be good enough.

## Peer Pressure

- Do not associate with people who want to change you.
- Always strive to be comfortable with yourself.
- Don't compare yourself to others (friends, family, models, magazine advertisements, etc.).
- Remember you are beautiful inside and outside, just the way you are. Don't let anyone convince you otherwise.
- Lose weight because it is in the best interest of your health, not because someone says you should.
- Learn to pay attention when someone is bullying you.
- Don't be a victim.
- If it sounds too good to be true, it probably is.
- Learn to trust and depend on your instincts.

## Some Characteristics of Bullies

- Bullies need to feel like they have control of their situation.
- Bullies speak badly towards and about others.
- Bullies want their own way most of the time.
- Bullies believe they have power over others.
- Bullies do not care what others think of them.

147

- Bullies don't often realize how much they hurt others.
- Bullies verbally hurt with their words by using name calling.
- Bullies intimidate using scare tactics.
- Bullies often hit and hurt others.
- Bullies might have been bullied themselves at some time in their lives.

Some Characteristics of Victims

- Feeling afraid.
- Feeling down.
- Feeling anxious.
- Feeling hopeless.
- Feeling physically sick.
- Feeling depressed.
- Feeling immobilized.
- Feeling worthless.
- Feeling incompetent.
- Feeling lethargic.
- Turning to drugs, alcohol, sex, or food to self-medicate pain.

## Healthy Weight Loss

Have you ever stepped on your bathroom scale and heard yourself yell, "I can't take it anymore!" Or maybe it was more like, "I just can't go on another diet!" Perhaps it was, "How can that number be right? My scale must be broken." Maybe it was even the all-time classic, "The dryer shrank my clothes again."

Are you a diet professional? Have you been on so many diets hoping and knowing this time will be different? Have you ever lost weight only to have it creep back on before you even knew that you had lost it? If any of this sounds familiar, you are not alone.

I have been on my own weight loss journey for what seems like my entire life. Years ago I weighed over 300 pounds. I had to learn that dieting did not work. Dieting made me more preoccupied with food, obsessed with the number on the scale, and I had feelings of guilt and shame when my dieting failed. Eating too few calories slowed down my metabolism and made it hard to lose weight. Eating too many calories added weight. I kept telling myself, "Just eat less and move more, and you will lose weight." That did not really work well for me, so I eventually started making weight loss wishes on birthday cakes, mine and the birthday cakes of everyone else. Needless to say, that did not work well either.

I had knowledge of calories, carbohydrates, and fat grams. I could count calories like I was a human abacus. However, this knowledge did not guarantee a weight loss for me. As a matter of fact, all that knowledge often caused me more stress and more guilt. I would say things to myself like, "I know what to do, so just do it. I'm a smart person and can do this once I put my mind to it. I would have lost weight by now if I had money for proper diet food or a diet program." I had intense feelings of guilt, disappointment, and disgust.

It really hurts to not succeed when trying to do everything right. The harder I tried, the more trapped, frustrated, and hopeless I felt. So what do you do when feelings of shame, guilt, and hopelessness make you want to give up and throw in the towel for good?

FIRST: Explore what drives your overeating habits. Ask the hard questions. Do you eat when you are happy, sad, stressed, hurt, bored, scared, mad, overspending or overscheduled? Perhaps you overeat out of habit because there is Halloween candy or free party food at your fingertips. Identify what and when you overeat and make note of the feelings as you are trying to submerge them. For me, each feeling was attached to either salty, sweet, or savory flavors, and I knew what foods I wanted to keep me from feeling something hurtful or painful.

SECOND: Understand diets do not work. Behavioral changes that can last a lifetime are what works. Reject the diet mentality. Learn when your body is actually hungry. You may not remember what being physically hungry really feels like and may need to relearn this feeling. Make peace with food because food is your friend and needs to be used wisely.

THIRD: According to the University of Maryland Medical Center, a relatively inactive female weighing 200 pounds eats between 2,000 and 2,300 calories daily to maintain this weight. However, a moderately active woman weighing 200 pounds eats 2,400 to 2,700 calories daily to maintain this weight. The rule of thumb is approximately 10 calories per pound per day when inactive and 12 calories per pound per day for people who are moderately active to maintain their current weight. A pound of fat contains roughly 3,500 calories, so provided your weight is currently stable, you should aim to reduce your current calorie intake by 500 calories per day if you want to lose one pound per week.

## Job Interviewing Tips

Job interviews can be nerve racking. We are told, "Try to think of the interviewers as ordinary people who are just like us." The difference is they have jobs, and we want a job. Then we are told, "Don't come across as desperate." How does a person not come across as desperate? The truth is many people are desperate when trying to get a job or find a better job.

Most people go to an interview at some time in their lives. Why? It is because employers want a chance to get to know their applicants. Of course they want to know if the applicant has the necessary job skills for the position, but more importantly they want to be assured the person they are hiring will be a good fit with their organization. For example, employers may be asking themselves:

- Is the applicant easy to talk to?
- Did the applicant arrive on time for the interview?
- Did the applicant come across as cocky?
- Is the applicant confident?
- Can the applicant look me in the eye?
- Did the applicant actually listen to what was being asked and then answer the question?
- Did the applicant come prepared?
- Is the applicant dressed properly?

In addition to determining if the job seeker has the much needed job skills, many employers are looking for people who are polite, well mannered, hardworking, and easy to be around. They want people who will represent their organization in a positive way. I have been on many interview panels and have listened to hundreds of applicants. I cannot emphasize enough the importance of being authentic. In other words, be yourself.

Besides being yourself, be sure to stress your strengths and positive attributes. Many people fail to do this because they feel they are bragging. This is not bragging. You are providing important information the employer needs to make an informed decision on who to hire. For example, if you are a hard worker who arrives at work 15 minutes early, then say so. If you are attending night school to acquire extra skills and knowledge, then be sure to let the interviewer know this. If you have particular skills that you feel are applicable to the job you are applying for, say so.

Remember, your job is to help the employer see who you are as a candidate and future employee in the organization. Think about your strengths before the interview, prepare and practice what you want to say, and then share the information with the employer. The employer wants to know you will be an asset. Interviews are the perfect platform to tell your story.

During the interview, try to determine if this is really the type of organization you would like to work for. Creating a good match is important on both sides of the interview table. What is the point of being fake, then taking a position that does not suit you in an organization where you don't really want to work? That's just it. There is no point. Start out being your authentic self from day one, and you never have to worry about being fake.

Here are some interview tips:

- Research the organization and the position you are applying for.
- Rehearse what you want to say.

- Dress properly for your interview. This means dressing one step up from the job you're applying for.
- Use good manners and always be polite.
- Maintain good eye contact and have a good handshake.
- Show confidence not arrogance.
- Cover up tattoos.
- Turn your cell phone off, and this does not mean put it on vibrate.
- Be positive.
- Carefully listen to and actually answer the questions being asked.
- Always be yourself.
- Believe there is a job out there for you.
- Don't quit!

# Epilogue

When everything in life seems out of control and difficult to manage, that's when it is crucial to make lots of room for hope. My pregnancy got off to a rocky start, but giving birth to Jeffrey was one of the best things that ever happened to me. Even though I am Jeffrey's mother, I am proud to say he is one of my very best friends, and I could not be prouder of him.

At the age of 20, Jeffrey enlisted in the United States Army and continues to proudly serve our country. Last year he was awarded the Bronze Star for meritorious service in a combat zone in Afghanistan. He is married to a girl he has known since childhood, and she is the love of his life. They have a 13 year old son who attends middle school, and last year he was inducted into the National Junior Honor Society for having a GPA higher than 3.75.

Jeffrey does not remember his early childhood trauma from when we lived with his dad, but he vividly remembers the trauma from living with Paul. Because of the trauma he has experienced, he is on his own personal journey of recovery. His goal is and always has been to be a good person, a good husband, and a good father to his son and their two dogs, Max and Tucker.

Jimmy returned to Tennessee and has been estranged from his son for over 20 years. While writing this book, I learned that Paul died about 12 years ago, but I do not know the cause of death.

As for me, I have had a long and rewarding career helping others grow into being the best version of themselves. My life experience combined with my Master of Science degree in Counselor Education has made it possible for me to be successful in my life coaching business.

Personally, my priority in life is to keep myself centered the best I can. Daily I use my head, my heart, and my gut approach to decision making. I find it is not always easy because sometimes people get disappointed when I say no to their requests. I still sometimes get a stomach ache when someone is upset with me, but I am not willing to give up my voice in an attempt to make other people happy.

Working on my own legacy is important because it is something I get to control. One of my goals is to add joy and laughter to the world. I want people to smile when they see me coming, not cringe and wonder if my mood will be good or bad.

Tom is the love of my life, and he joined me on my journey of recovery nearly 30 years ago. He is a wonderful man who works on his own personal growth and development daily. We have made a happy life together, and without his love and support this book would not have been possible. He knows emotional safety is important to me, and when I feel emotionally safe I am the best version of myself. I have always said the best thing about being in a relationship with Tom is I get to be me in the relationship. He has always encouraged me to be myself.

No matter how bad life seems there is hope for something better, but you have to work hard to make healthy changes in your life. I had to learn how to do my own emotional work with a therapist. Then I had to admit to myself I was a big part of my own problems. Taking ownership of my participation in my own problems was not fun. I wanted to blame other people for my choices and my misery. If I did not want to continue to be a victim, I had to do something different.

I live close to my Dad who moved back to Fair Oaks nearly two years ago. Dad comes over for a visit and a morning cup of coffee about five days each week, and I enjoy the time we spend together. I don't hold grudges and don't have the need to bring up the hurtful parts of the past. I did my work, and Jeffrey and I survived.

After my mom's death, my sister Anna, her husband of over 30 years, and their 10 year old daughter moved into the family home my parents built.

I felt like Mom's foster parents were my grandparents until the day they died. Mom got lucky when she was placed with a caring family who loved her dearly. They were role models and helped break the cycle of abuse in her life. Mom got to see how a loving family lives and treats one another, and I got the benefit of her experiences.

My Grandpa Frank married again and had a daughter named Victoria. Mom and Victoria became very close friends as children and they remained close until the day Victoria died three years ago. She was my loving aunt from the moment I was born and played a significant part in my life. I love and miss her dearly.

You never know for sure how your life will turn out. My mom was able to find her voice as a child. She listened to her head, her heart and her gut, and then she created a new legacy for herself. She created a life she wanted for herself instead of keeping the life her family of origin had offered her. She did not allow revenge, hatred, and ugliness to take over her heart and soul. She was one tough lady, and I am proud to use her as my role model.

I always say you act like the people you associate with, so you better be associating with people you want to act like. Find people you admire and spend time with them and see what happens. I love being around people I admire because this makes me feel better from the inside out. Most of the time the people don't even know I am using them as role models.

In spite of everything you may have been through, remember you are capable of finding your own sense of inner peace and joy.

I know for sure:

*If you believe you are worthy you will be.*

*If you want your legacy to be powerful, it can be.*

*If you want to be fulfilled in a personal manner, do the work because you're worth it.*

*Be The Best You-You Can Be!*

## Suggested Reading

Susan Jeffers, Ph.D., *Feel the Fear and Do It Anyway*, (First Ballantine Books, 1988).

Joshua C. Klapow, Ph.D. and Sheri D. Pruitt, Ph.D, *Living Smart*, (DiaMedica Publishing, 2008).

Harold H. Bloomfield, M.D. and Robert K. Cooper, Ph.D. *The Power of 5*, (St. Martins Press, 1994).

Pam Peeke, M.D., MPH, FACP, *The Hunger Fix*, (Rodale Inc. 2012).

Frank Bruni, *Born Round*, (Penguin Press, 2009).

Follow Julie's Blog @
www.woodworkerlifecoaching.com

87302444R00095

Made in the USA
San Bernardino, CA
03 September 2018